A Horseman's Handb

GH00362829

Carol Green
Stable Management Explained

Ward Lock Limited · London

Horseman's Handbooks

© Carol Green 1977
Paperback ISBN 0-7063-6408-2

First published in Great Britain in 1977
by Ward Lock Limited, 82 Gower Street,
London WC1E 6EQ, an Egmont Company.
Reprinted 1979, 1981, 1985

Cover photograph: Peter Loughran

Text set in Times by
Computacomp (UK) Limited,
Fort William

Printed and bound in Great Britain by
Hollen Street Press, Slough

1   Introduction: stable construction

This book is intended to be of assistance both to the owner groom
and to the trainee student in the care and management of the
horse. Costs today are constantly rising, and the average horse-
lover should be able to care properly for his one or two horses,
becoming confident of being able to ride, school, feed and
generally look after his own horse.

Many people needing to stable a horse for the first time have to
make the best of whatever is available locally, and find a yard or
stable that has already been built. You may perhaps be renting a
box, paddock or field. Or you may have the opportunity of
building your own little stable yard. I am thinking now of an ideal
situation where you have decided to buy your own horse, and can
plan a stable yard first of all, even before you have a horse. I hope,
however, that these ideas will also provide some guidelines to
those who want to improve on what is already there.

When first considering the building of a stable yard it is
important to take into account the type of soil upon which one
should try to build. Dry foundations, with easy access to a good
supply of fresh water, are essential. An area that is light, allowing
good drainage and fresh air, is of course most important for the
health of your horse. The best type of soil upon which to build is
gravel or deep sand, as this provides a firm base, natural drainage
and dryness; chalk, limestone or granite are also suitable. Try to
avoid marshy land, heavy clay or peaty soils. If it is really
necessary to build upon any of these types of soil, then I would
strongly recommend that you first lay down a base of subsoil to
help create natural drainage to the earth; solid foundations for the
stables are important. It is better to make all artificial bases wider
than the building itself, as the structure will thus be more rigid. A
well-planned drainage system is an essential factor, particularly if

your buildings are erected in an area where subsoil has been used. If the land is very damp, then it is better to raise the buildings on solid arches.

The loose-boxes themselves should be erected where it is possible for them to receive the maximum amount of sun and fresh air and yet be protected from the winds of the north-east and north-west. Horses drink a great deal of water; it is therefore important that running water is laid on to each building so that each loose-box, the tack room and feed room have water readily available. It is not really necessary for every loose-box to have running water; in planning a large yard you should allow for an outside tap at every three boxes or so. If you need to build, and have only one horse, it would be a good idea to try and find others to share the cost. Horses are happier in company, and you will probably find you save some of the cost by building one larger yard rather than several small ones. The size of the loose-box is important. A box some 4m by 4.3m (12ft by 14ft) will accommodate comfortably a large hunter or event horse. Ponies can manage in smaller boxes, some 3m by 4m (10ft by 12ft).

Ventilation is an important aspect of the design of stables. The stable door is best made in two parts, so that it is a simple matter to keep the upper door open and thus ensure a good supply of fresh air. If windows are incorporated, then they are best built into the same wall as the door, so that draughts are avoided. Wooden louvre boards fitted high in the stable wall, just below the roof, are useful outlets for stale air.

For the sake of safety, it is very important that the stable roof is made of a fire-proof material. The roof is best made in a sloping design as this will afford good ventilation, and give a natural air space and light. A sloping roof should run from front to back. The slope of the roof may extend so that there is an overhang of between 1.2m–1.5m (4ft–5ft), which will provide shelter from the rain and sun.

Windows should open inwards in a sloping fashion so the fresh air entering is directed upwards before gently coming down and circulating through the stable, spreading throughout the box to avoid the possibility of draughts.

6

The choice of stable floor is largely a matter of personal preference, though some points should be borne in mind when considering the best type for any particular purpose. The floor must be hard, non-slip and allow all liquid to drain away freely. Typical materials are Staffordshire bricks, concrete, clay, tiles and wood. To my mind, without doubt, Staffordshire bricks make the best type of floor; they are long-lasting, allow good drainage and are reliably non-slip. I am hesitant to advise the use of concrete, as although I know it to be very inexpensive and widely used, it does tend to become rather slippery if neglected. If concrete is used, however, make sure that it is well maintained and always kept a little rough on the surface to prevent the horse losing his balance in the stable when turning. Clay can make a good floor if it is readily available. It must be kept well beaten down and flattened and then it can work quite well. Tiles, although attractive, tend to become slippery with the horse constantly turning about in the stable. A wooden floor is adequate but it must always be meticulously well cared for, as wood is naturally inclined to rot and splinter.

As few fittings as possible should be built into each box. I like to have just a ring at eye level for tying up a hay net and another ring nearby for tying up the horse. I prefer not to have a fitted manger, water-holder or hayrack, as I feel that the fewer projections the better; there is less chance of injury to the horse. Some stables have automatic watering systems, and if you are building your boxes from scratch you may like to have such a system installed. Each stable has its own automatic water supply, and the horse operates it as he requires. There are both good and bad points to this system. In summer it is generally very reliable, but under cold winter conditions the water tends to freeze. It is also difficult to establish how much water the horse is drinking, and since water is the important factor in the health and condition of the horse, it is useful to be able to keep an eye on his intake of it. For this reason I tend to be a little old-fashioned, and prefer to have water buckets in the stable. I usually leave my horses with two buckets of water, ensuring their access to a plentiful supply all the time; it is quite simple to replenish the buckets at regular intervals to prevent contamination by ammonia fumes.

In designing the tack room remember it must be light and, above all, damp proof. An electric heater should be installed to maintain an even temperature. The feed room should be dry and vermin proof, and both areas should be easily accessible. The organization of the feed room needs careful thought and attention. All food should be kept dry in a metal container with a sealed lid, which should be raised off the floor as a protection from damp, mice and rust; new dustbins serve the purpose very well. A chart with the amount of food that each horse or pony has to eat should be clearly visible in the feed room and should be kept up to date. If this policy is strictly followed and you should happen to be absent at any time, it is easy for someone else to feed according to your routine. It is advisable to have a pair of scales so that food may be measured and weighed, and a scoop to measure the feed is also useful. A small cupboard to hold salt, mineral additives, tonics, and medicines that need to be put into a particular feed is another convenient item.

If you are not in a position to build your own stables, to rent a stable or to keep your horse at a livery stable, there is no need to be deterred from keeping a horse. With care and energy it is possible to keep a horse in a field or paddock, and I will discuss this later on in the book (see page 40 onwards).

The feed room. Notice the large metal containers, which keep the food dry and free from vermin

2   Bedding

Let us now consider the question of bedding for the stabled horse. Before the horse may be put in his stable, something must be put upon the floor. A good deep bed is essential to the comfort, warmth and general well-being of a horse. If he is compelled always to stand when at rest it is inevitable that his limbs will suffer; constant standing could well lead to 'filled' (that is, swollen), legs, fatigue and a general loss of health and condition.

The main types of bedding are straw, sawdust or wood shavings, peat moss, and shredded paper. Use good quality straw, preferably an old straw; short straw is generally the more popular variety, and is more economical than long straw. The excellence of straw for bedding lies in its good drainage characteristics and the fact that it is easily disposed of. You may be able to use some of the manure on your own garden, and larger quantities can be sold to mushroom growers, market gardeners, etc. The traditional form of bedding has always been straw, and it is, I think, still one of the nicest forms. Wheat straw is the best to use for horses, though it could be barley, wheat or oat. The disadvantage of oat straw is that horses tend to eat it. It is very palatable and you may well find that your bedding will disappear very quickly. Barley is not so comfortable for horses, as the awns are slightly prickly and can irritate the skin, particularly of better-bred horses, which have more sensitive skins. The other thing I dislike about barley is that it too may be eaten; it is not very good for horses and can give them colic. Try to buy your straw direct from a reliable farmer; you will almost certainly be able to buy it more cheaply than if you go to a merchant. Learn to recognize good straw from bad: wheat straw should be a clear golden colour, dry, rustling and crisp — not greyish, damp or mouldy at the centre of the bale. Sawdust used for bedding must be dry, and it is an absorbent form of bedding but will block drains unless precautions are taken in advance. Although beds made of sawdust are easy to keep clean and easy to handle, sawdust does create a disposal problem and it is often necessary to burn it at home. Peat moss, on the other hand, is valuable manure for gardeners, and it is therefore easier to dispose of. Peat moss is darker in colour than sawdust or wood shavings, and it presents a similar problem in being an absorbent form of bedding. Shredded paper is particularly useful when a horse is allergic or sensitive to dust.

The haynet shown here is tied at the correct level for the horse's comfort. Notice also the good, deep bed of straw and the water bucket securely fixed in the corner so that the horse cannot upset it while drinking.

3   The daily routine

Mucking out — the job of cleaning out the stables — should be done early in the morning. The tools required for mucking out are a pitchfork, a spade, a four-pronged fork with a short handle, a wheelbarrow, and a broom. The pitchfork is used for shaking the straw and arranging the bed so that it is level in the centre, with deep banks around the edge. A spade will be necessary only to pick up heavy droppings on a sawdust or a peat-moss bed. A four-pronged fork is useful for removing droppings from all types of bed and the wheelbarrow for carrying them out of the stable area; the broom will of course be used to sweep the stable floor.

The procedure for mucking out a straw bed is first to tie up the horse with a headcollar. Remove all droppings that can be seen on the surface, shaking the straw as you pick them up. Starting at the door, put the clean straw to one side of the box. I find it easiest to throw the clean straw to the side of the box away from the door. Shaking the straw should cause the soiled straw to fall through the prongs of the fork. The floor must be swept clean every day, and should be disinfected once a week. To bed down for the horse it is best to shake the straw thoroughly, and add more straw as necessary. It is important to make sure that the bed is deep in the middle with good banks around the sides, so when the horse moves around or lies down the floor is really well covered to prevent any chance of injury. It is much quicker to deal with a sawdust or wood-shaving bed. Tie up the horse, remove all the droppings and wet patches with a fork, rake the sides to the middle and put more sawdust on the top. Having removed all soiled bedding to your muck heap remember to stack the manure into a rectangular pile, banking up the outer sides and keep the heap tidy. In this way it is easier for collection, and also rots better for use on the garden.

I believe that all stable floors, whether the horse is normally bedded down on straw or on sawdust, need to be well scrubbed at regular intervals. The stable should be washed thoroughly with strong disinfectant, particular attention being paid to the floor, then hosed down and left to air and dry. This should be done at least once a week. Stable tools should also be kept hygienic and in good working order. I feel that it is best to clean them every day, and hang them on a wall with the prongs and broomheads in the air. In this way they are kept in a clean and tidy fashion, are always quick to hand, and are far less likely to wear out quickly than if left standing or lying on the floor. Of course in a yard where horses are moving about it is unwise — and could be very dangerous — to allow any tools to be left lying about. I have seen a horse severely injured by an accident with a stable fork.

Some readers may be familiar with the use of a skep (manure basket), an item which unfortunately seems to have gone out of fashion. Skeps used to be found, and should still be found, in every well-run yard so that even with one stable and one horse it is an important article and should be in position outside the stable. A skep is a small basket, (I use a plastic laundry basket) which is kept close to the stable, so that a person entering the stable and finding a dropping can quickly remove it into the skep. This is, of course, a useful way of saving straw, and I suspect it is largely due to laziness that more people do not use a skep and follow this worthwhile and economical practice. With costs perpetually rising I hope that the use of skeps may become fashionable again, to the furthering of good stable management and the additional benefit of better care and attention to the animals' feet.

Now we come to the important subject of the daily routine. I recommend that you adopt a routine which is practical for you to follow regularly; all horses, by nature creatures of habit, thrive on a regular routine. The programme outlined here is ideally suited to a healthy stable-fed, 16-hand horse in hard condition, hunting three days a fortnight. I have also indicated approximate amounts as a guide for feeding (see page 32), and reasons for adjusting the amount. I have found this routine works very well; adapt it to suit your needs, so that you can maintain it easily and regularly.

Daily Timetable

7.00 a.m. Down to stable, general inspection.
Feed small haynet 2kg (4lb) if not exercising early, and 1.6kg (3$\frac{1}{2}$lb) corn with bran. Water, sweep, muck out. Throw up rug and 'quarter'.

9.30 a.m. Remove rugs, tack up, exercise for two hours.

11.30 a.m. Return, tack off, water (always in box) rack up, remove droppings and strap well. Day rugs on, refill water bucket, fill haynet 2.7kg (6lb). Tidy yard.

12.30 p.m. Second feed (1.6kg or 3$\frac{1}{2}$lb corn with bran and carrots), tie up haynet, leave horse in peace.

4.30 p.m. Remove droppings, pick out feet, fill up water bucket, remove day rugs and put on night rugs. Clean tack, then feed (2.1kg or 4$\frac{1}{2}$lb corn with bran, carrots). Tie up haynet (3.6kg or 8lb). Tidy yard.

8.00 p.m. General inspection, check rugs, buckets, beds, hay. Shut up for the night — if mild weather, leave top stable door open to allow plenty of fresh air.

Let us follow through the routine as a whole before looking in more detail at the aspects of it which you may not have experienced before. Begin your day at 7.00 a.m., go down to the stable and make a general inspection of your horse: check that he has not suffered any injuries during the night; adjust his rugs if they have slipped; notice whether he has drunk all his water, and has eaten all his hay.

Give the horse a small net of approximately 2kg (4lb) hay, tie him up and prepare to begin the first routine, which is to take the water buckets out of the stable and to scrub them out, to muck out the stable by removing all the droppings and soiled straw, and setting fair the bed. I do not like to leave my horses standing on a stone floor so, having mucked out, I will then put the bed down again so the horse has something to stand on. Refill your water buckets and put them in the corner of the stable. Make sure the

14

horse has the opportunity to drink if he wishes. Throw up (that is, remove) the rug and 'quarter' the horse. 'Quartering' is the quick grooming of the horse in the early morning: any soiled stains can be removed from his coat; his mane and tail are brushed out; hay, straw or wood shavings that have stuck in his coat are removed; his feet are picked out and he is generally tidied. This is not a thorough grooming but just enough to make him look respectable while being exercised.

When the horse is tidy then he may be given a small corn feed, for the average 16-hand horse in full work, 1.6kg ($3^1/_2$lb) of corn with approximately 220g ($^1/_2$lb) bran might be the right feed. Depending on my horse's temperament I might substitute the corn with horse and pony cubes (nuts) or racehorse cubes, or make a composition feed of nuts and oats. The horse should be given plenty of time to eat his food and digest it before being asked to go out on exercise — at least an hour should pass after he has finished eating. This allows him plenty of time to digest it properly and will help prevent him from getting colic. Having made sure that the horse is feeding comfortably, you can then go and have your own breakfast.

Returning to the horse at around 9.30 a.m., remove the rugs, tack him up and prepare to exercise him. Because the horse is hunting fit he will probably need to be exercised for approximately two hours, not of fast but of steady work, including hill and road work to harden his legs and tendons. On returning to the stable after exercise, making sure that he is cool by the time the stables are reached, remove his tack and offer him a drink of water. Tie him up short (with a quick-release knot for safety), remove any droppings from the stable and then strap him well. Strapping is the name given to the thorough and complete grooming of the horse (see page 25). Having groomed him well, put his rug on, refill his water bucket and give him a small net of hay — of approximately 2.2kg (5lb). If my yard had become a little untidy I would probably do odd jobs around the yard at this point, and tidy it up. I might even clean tack. At 12.30 p.m. the horse should be given his second feed of the day, which would again consist of 1.6kg ($3^1/_2$lb) of concentrated food, with bran, and perhaps some chopped carrots. I would then leave the horse in peace. The horse can be left until 4.30 p.m. when another visit is needed to remove the droppings, fill the water buckets, pick out the horse's feet, remove his day rug and put on his night rug, clean the tack, and then give the horse another feed. The larger feed would probably consist of 2.1kg (4^1/$_2$lb) concentrated feed with bran and carrots. I would then tie up a haynet and tidy up my yard. At 8.00 p.m. in the evening there should be a last inspection to check his rug, buckets, hay and bed, and to shut him up for the night. If the horse was having extra short feeds I might at this time give him another one. If it was a mild evening I would leave the top half of the stable door open — the weather has to be really very cold for me to shut the top door. If the horse was laid up or not hunting and his work was cut down, the hard food, such as corn, would be reduced. One must remember to feed according to the work, age and temperament of the horse. If the horse is lame or ill, then he must be put on a laxative diet and rested. (A laxative diet is a diet which contains almost no protein, and the horse has his corn ration severely cut.)

I would like to go into the general inspection of a horse in more detail, and consider how to study his general health and condition when you look at him first thing in the morning. The horse should appear at a glance to be healthy and relaxed, his bed should appear relatively undisturbed, his water bucket should be half full, and his haynet empty. There should be no signs of any injury to his limbs. A horse is said to be in good condition when he is well covered, though not fat. His head, neck and quarters should be firm with the skin moving over them freely. He should look alert and have a good gloss on his coat, which should feel smooth to the touch. His eyes should be bright, the lining to the eyes and mouth should be salmon pink in colour. A horse in good condition is capable of doing all the work that is required of him, performing all his tasks without undue stress or strain. This situation is obtained by regular feeding and exercise, coupled with good grooming and regular care for the horse's teeth. A horse that looks dull in his eye, has a staring coat, is thin and off his food, listless and generally in poor condition, needs immediate attention. It could be due to mal-

This horse is in good condition. It is easy to see that he looks
alert, his coat is blooming, and he is well muscled

This horse is in poor condition. His ribs are visible, he lacks
muscle, and his coat is dull

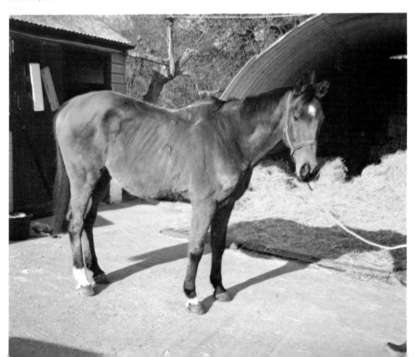

The stable buildings must have good guttering, with the
windows placed high up and opening inwards. The metal grille
over the window prevents the horse from injuring himself on
the glass. No electric cables or switches are fitted inside the stable

nutrition, teeth problems, worms, bad digestion or anaemia. If the horse is suffering from any of these ailments then your attention must be given straight away. You should seek the advice of your vet as soon as possible. Get the vet to check the horse's teeth and possibly ask him to take a blood sample. The horse will require regular worming and the vet should be consulted about this and a suitable diet. If the horse is very malnourished, your vet may suggest you feed him on flesh-producing foods; such as linseed, barley, beans and peas, and perhaps sugar-beet pulp. However, it will normally take three to four months, depending on the horse, before there is any apparent improvement in his condition. It may also be necessary to feed a vitamin and mineral supplement to correct any deficiencies or imbalances.

Handling your horse

For inspection of the horse in the morning and at all other times, it will be necessary for you to be familiar with the correct way to handle him. Bad handling or ill treatment will spoil any animal; no matter how perfect a horse or pony you think you may have bought, you will spoil him very quickly if you do not have good horse sense. Conversely, good handling and correct treatment will in time improve a difficult horse. Successful handling of animals depends largely on the person dealing with them having plenty of patience, tact, kindness, and firmness, coupled with good common sense. When entering the stable speak to the horse softly in an encouraging tone, as horses are sensitive to the tone of the human voice. Approach him on the left, the 'near' side, walking towards his shoulder. Pat him and speak again. Do not rush or bustle; all hasty, hurried movements around the horse must be avoided, particularly if he is a young or nervous creature. When handling or grooming try to stand close to the horse as this will give him confidence, and there is less chance of you getting hurt. The end of a kick or strike is the real danger; if you are close to the horse you will suffer only a push, with less risk of injury to yourself.

Having entered the stable you will probably wish to put a halter or headcollar on the horse and tie him up. The best way to do this is again to approach him from the near side and speak to him. Pat him gently at the same time, slipping the rope attached to the headcollar round his neck so that he is secured. Bring the noseband up onto his head and the headpiece over the poll and then fasten it comfortably. When the headcollar is correctly fitted tie the horse up, using a quick-release knot.

Having tied up your horse you will want to muck him out. I have dealt with mucking out a straw bed on page 12. If you use wood shavings or shredded paper, the method is even easier. Simply go into the stable and remove any droppings that are evident on top of the bedding and any wet patches, fork over and shake the whole; then rake it nice and flat and put fresh bedding on top. Peat moss is a little more difficult to handle, as it is heavier and darker in colour, and I find it best to take out the droppings as soon as you can and maintain the bed on a 'deep-litter' system. This involves making a fairly good depth of bed at first — about 15cm (6in) deep. Instead of mucking out every day just take off the top droppings and wet patches, rake the whole bed very thoroughly and add more peat moss in a deeper bank round the sides, with some more on top of the bed itself if you think necessary. The banked sides prevent the horse from getting an injury such as a capped hock or elbow, by rolling too vigorously in the box. I think a wheat straw bed is the nicest to work with and the best for the horse, but if you have disposal problems or you find that you have easier access to peat or to wood shavings, then they are probably worth the extra trouble. They are fairly quick to muck out initially but you must remove all the droppings every time you enter the stable, and keep the bed very well raked and shaken so it always smells sweet and pleasant to the horse.

A simpler routine for office workers

I do hope that readers who work in an office, or have to go away to their business each day are not discouraged so far. It is quite easy to work out a simpler routine than the one already proposed, that will enable you to spend less time with the horse each day and still give him proper care and attention.

However, the most important point to remember is that the horse thrives on a routine and there is therefore nothing to stop you going to the stables first thing in the morning at 6.00 or 6.30 a.m., checking over your horse, making sure he has suffered no injury or discomfort in the night and, instead of feeding the horse, get him ready for exercise straight away. Having exercised him, return to the stable to brush him over quickly so that he is comfortable and left with no sweat marks on him, and then pick up the bed. If you are going to manage your horse by this method, you may not have time to muck him out thoroughly. In this case, you could adopt the deep-litter system, where you just remove the wet, soiled patches, keeping the dry bedding and adding fresh bedding when required. This method is considerably quicker. You may ask 'Why isn't it done all the time?' The reason is that the bedding has to be layered and removed entirely, usually on your weekend off, and started again. But you could quite easily keep the horse on a deep-litter system with great success. On your return to the stable, having made sure he has access to water, given him a brush, and set fair the bed, then give him a small amount of hay (about 1kg or 2–3lb) to help him masticate properly and encourage him to be in a relaxed state of mind after his ride and while you tidy him up. Having done all this I would put the tack away, ensure the yard was tidy, and leave the horse with a short feed in a manger hung by its brackets to the outside of the stable door. The horse can then put his head over the door and eat from the securely fixed manger. These mangers are very helpful if you can't be with the horse the whole time, since it is difficult for the horse to turn his feed over and so waste his feed, and this type of container cannot injure the horse during your absence.

It is vital that your horse has water — two full buckets — so that he has access to water all morning. Your horse should be looked at again at lunchtime, when he should be watered, any droppings removed, and fed. This will be a hard feed consisting of about 1kg (2–3lb) of oats, a little bran and perhaps some horse and pony cubes. I will talk about feeding in detail in Chapter 5. I would also give him a 2kg (5lb) haynet to keep him going until the evening. If you are unable to check on your horse at lunchtime, he will probably manage quite well on two regular feeds a day.

If the time of year allows, or it is fairly mild weather and you have a paddock available to you, then I would turn your horse out for two or three hours a day. This is very helpful if you don't always have time to exercise him properly. Sometimes I find two friends can work together, one friend coping with the horse early in the morning, and the other taking over in the evening.

When you return to your horse in the evening about 6.00 p.m., this is the time when effort on your part is needed, because the horse is dependent on you. So check again that he has suffered no injury, that he is perfectly well and just as you left him. Notice how much water he has drunk, if he has eaten all his hay, if his bed has been disturbed in any way, and if his rugs have slipped or moved and need adjusting. Having noted all these points and corrected them as necessary, you may need first of all to tie up your horse and to set fair the bed. This means to remove any droppings, and in the case of the peat-moss and wood-shavings bed it may be necessary to rake it to make it tidy for the evening. In the straw bed there may be soiled patches which have to be removed, so shake up the bed, set it fair, banking up the sides and making sure that it is reasonably deep in the middle, so that when the horse moves round he is not going to paw a hole in the middle of the floor, lie down to sleep and then perhaps injure himself.

It is important at this time of day to give your horse a thorough grooming session for a minumum of twenty minutes. For details of this routine, known as 'strapping', see page 25. Once you have re-rugged him, give your horse a small feed (about 1kg or 2–3lb mixture of oats, bran and cubes). After this, leave him to eat his feed and go and clean his tack. It is a good idea to go back and make sure that he is comfortable for the night, that he had eaten his feed properly and had plenty of water. Finally leave him with 5–8kg (10–15lb) of hay according to the size of your horse, in a net for the night.

NOTE Feed quantities given in this chapter are meant as a rough guide. However these amounts can vary enormously from horse to horse, depending on individual circumstances. For more advice on feeding, see Chapter 5.

4 Grooming

Now I want to go a little more deeply into the subject of grooming. I have already mentioned that if you are keeping your horse in peak form it is essential for his health, condition, cleanliness and appearance that he is well groomed each day. Grooming tools number about ten or so and are as follows:

A *hoof pick*, which is used for cleaning the feet. A *dandy brush* which removes the mud and grease, but must be used very gently on thin-skinned horses as it is rather hard and rough, and must *never* be used on the mane and tail as it can split the hair. The *body brush* is used on the body, mane and tail to remove scurf and grease from the coat. The *curry comb* is used to clean the body

The grooming kit. From the left, top row: water brush, tail bandage, mane and tail comb, scissors, (for trimming the feathers on the heels) two sponges, hoof pick, hoof oil; bottom row: body brush, metal curry comb, rubber curry comb, wisp and dandy brush

How the wisp is twisted into shape

brush. The *water brush* is used to dampen the mane and tail, causing them to lie flat. The *two sponges*, one for cleaning the eyes and nose, the other for cleaning the dock (it is better to have them of different colours so that you can easily distinguish them). The *mane and tail comb* is used primarily for pulling. It is important not to be rough with the comb as it is possible to split and tear the hair. The *stable rubber* gives a final polish to the horse after grooming. The *wisp* is used to build up muscle and promote circulation.

The wisp

The wisp is a worthwhile item and it is quite easy to make and use. First, soak some hay in a bucket of water. Then, with the help of a friend, twist the hay into a rope 2.7–4m (8–12ft) long. Dampen it again and cut off any frayed edges in the length of the rope. Make two loops at one end of the rope, twist the remainder of the rope in a figure of eight around the two loops until the rope has been used up, and then thread the end through the ends of the loops to fasten off. The wisp should be firm and large enough to sit in the hand comfortably.

It is a good idea to practise making wisps until you have really acquired the knack, as they are a valuable part of grooming equipment. The wisp is used to 'bang' the horse — bringing the wisp firmly and quite sharply down onto a muscular part of the horse. Begin by banging for two minutes on each side, increasing the amount a little each day. The fit hunter or event horse should

ideally receive forty minutes banging every day. The p~
which special attention should be paid are the neck and crest, the
forearm, shoulder, croup and quarters and second thigh. Be very
careful to avoid any bony or unprotected parts of the horse, such
as the loins. Introduce your horse gradually to banging in order
not to alarm him.

A grooming programme

As with all aspects of stable management good grooming (or
strapping, as it is called) is a matter of regular and closely followed
routine. I am going to give you a programme that can be followed
without any difficulty and I would recommend that you follow
this routine if you haven't groomed a horse very often, until it
becomes second nature. A grooming session should last for a
minimum of twenty minutes, but hopefully you may be able to
spend half an hour.

1   Collect your grooming kit. This should be kept together in a
container such as a suitable bag or box.

2   Put a headcollar or halter on the horse and tie him up short,
using a knot that will untie easily, that is, a quick-release
knot, which cannot be pulled too tight.

3   Pick out the feet with the hoof pick, taking each foot in turn,
and allow anything that may be lodged there to fall into the
skep.

4   Use the dandy brush to remove all the sweat and caked mud
from the body and legs. Begin at the poll on the near side and
work methodically over the body, taking particular care with
the saddle and girth area. If the horse is ticklish and
particularly sensitive, you can dispense with the dandy brush
and go on to the body brush.

5   The body brush and curry comb should be used next. Begin
at the poll on the near side and, using firm circular strokes,
work all over the horse to clean him really well. Every few
strokes you will need to clean the brush with the curry comb.
Although you should be sure to put more effort into the care
of the horse than the cleaning of the brush, do remember to

. the curry comb and then empty the
͵ing it into the skep on the floor.

The wisp should be slightly damp when you bring it down vigorously onto those parts of the horse where the muscles are hard and flat, such as the neck, shoulder, croup and thigh. It is a massage for the horse, and will promote his fitness and strengthen and develop his muscles.

7   Wring the sponges out in a bucket of clean water, and cleanse the eyes and nose with one, and cleanse the dock with the other, in that order.

8   Lay the mane firmly and smoothly over to one side (preferably the right side) by dipping the ends of the water brush into a bucket of water and then using it to dampen the mane. The tail should also be treated in this way.

9   Oil the hooves by using a small brush which is dipped in hoof oil for this purpose. This will both improve the appearance of the feet and lubricate them. The feet should be oiled on the wall (the outside of the hoof) and on the underside of the foot at the heels.

10   Finally, go over the horse with the stable rubber for a last polish and put on a tail bandage (see page 65).

Grooming the grass-kept horse

A programme similar to that outlined for the stabled horse should be followed for the horse that lives out at grass, although it is not necessary to groom so vigorously with the body brush and curry comb. The grass-kept horse needs the natural oil in his coat to protect him from the elements, so when grooming him pay particular attention to the cleaning of the feet, since stones are more likely to become lodged there, and improve his appearance by an all-over grooming with a dandy brush. It is still a good policy to prepare the mane and tail with a body brush because these split just as easily on the grass-kept horse as do those of the stable-kept horse, if roughly treated. It is refreshing for any horse to have his eyes, nose and dock sponged and it is, therefore, advisable for you to do so. The grass-kept horse will not be in the same hard condition as the stable-kept horse and so may not require wisping. In summer it is important to go over the horse very lightly every day with fly repellent or lotion; on a hot day a horse can be severely disturbed and worried by flies and it is an act of kindness to use some deterrent.

When you have groomed the horse thoroughly, you must re-rug him. Put on the under blanket first and then the top blanket, which will be your jute rug, and then the roller if your rugs do not have their own straps. I find it a good idea to have a piece of foam or sponge underneath the roller so that there is no risk of pressure on the withers of the horse. Then do up the buckles of the roller and finally do up the breast strap, that is, the buckle around the horse's chest. It is important to do it in this order because if you do up the front first and something startles your horse, the rugs will slip to the ground, still strapped around the horse's neck. This can frighten him or panic him even more, and he might tear your rugs in the process. So do remember to put the roller on first and then do up the rug.

Cleaning your grooming kit

It is important to keep your grooming kit clean and in good repair. It is obviously impossible to keep a horse clean if the equipment is dirty, excessively worn or damaged. The way to clean your kit is to wash the brushes in a bowl of warm water to which about a tablespoon of salt has been added. Try not to get wooden handles wet, as they will eventually rot. If the handles are made of leather, treat them carefully with saddle soap to keep them supple. A weekly wash in a saline solution should be enough. I am inclined to avoid the use of soap, as horses' skins are sensitive to it.

5 Foods, feeding and watering

It is essential that the horse has plenty of clean water available at all times, particularly before his feeds. Failure to observe this golden rule may result in an attack of colic and a general loss of condition. The horse's stomach is very small, and in his natural state at grass he will be slowly grazing all the time. It is therefore best to feed a stabled horse in small quantities, giving three or four feeds each day. The horse will be able to obtain the maximum benefit from his food, as he will have time to masticate and digest it properly. If, however, you do not have the time to give so many feeds, most horses can manage on two: one in the morning and one at night. After he has been fed a horse must be allowed at least an hour to rest before being asked to work or undertake anything strenuous.

The horse's solid diet should be well-balanced, and include a fair proportion of fats, starches, protein, vitamins and minerals for his growth and condition.

It is important to remember that every horse must be treated as an individual as far as feeding is concerned. When working out a suitable diet for your horse you must consider the breed of horse or pony, his temperament, the work that he will be required to do, his age, his likes and dislikes, and his ability to digest certain types of food.

Try to feed at the same time each day, making sure that the horse has plenty of bulk — hay or grass — in his diet. The diet will be even better if you feed him something succulent every day. For instance, it is a good idea to cut your horse some grass if he is stabled; carrots, apples and turnips are all good and welcome foods, but should be chopped into quite small pieces before being given to the horse.

See that only good quality food is given, in a clean utensil which will not tip over. So often one sees food wasted as soon as it is put out because the container is of an unsuitable shape and the horse in his impatience has kicked over the feed! It is a false economy to buy cheap lesser quality food, as horses are fastidious eaters and may well refuse it. If it is necessary to change your horse's diet — either to put him on a higher protein diet or to feed more bulk — try to make the change a gradual one so that he slides into the new routine without being fully aware of the change. He will maintain much better health and condition if you remember this.

Hay often varies in its goodness and value, depending on its type and age; when changing to a new hay mix it with the old stock. Think ahead when ordering food, and if you always pay for your feed orders promptly, you are more likely to enjoy a good service in return.

If a horse is ill and off work for some reason, then his protein diet must be stopped. Feed him a laxative diet consisting of hay, bran mashes, carrots, apples and the like.

Next, a few words about the types, qualities, purchasing and methods of feeding hay. There are two principal types: meadow hay, which is grown on a permanent pasture; and seed hay, which is a specially sown crop. Meadow hay is softer, very palatable and usually not as expensive as seed hay. The softness enables it to be digested easily by old horses, or those that are sick. Seed hay is very high in protein, is much stronger to handle and is difficult for old horses to digest. It is, however, very nutritious and is preferred by the young, strong, healthy animal. Most horses in hard work are fed seed hay. Seed hay, such as alfalfa, should be increased gradually and not introduced suddenly into the horse's diet.

Good quality hay should be dry, sweet-smelling, and with a good taste. It is from green to light brown in colour, and each bale will vary in weight (from about 18–20kg or 40–50lb), though the hay should not be tightly pressed. It is usually cheaper to buy your hay and straw in large quantities, and you might be able to buy a stack that is of good quality and store the hay yourself. Alternatively, if you have confidence in your farmer or feed merchant, buy the stack and have him deliver to you from it at regular intervals. This might be slightly more expensive than the first method but if you are short of space it will be more practical.

It is wise to buy enough hay to last you throughout the winter season, as hay becomes much more expensive after Christmas, and sometimes almost unobtainable.

Hay is best fed from a haynet, which keeps the hay off the ground and thus avoids waste. It is easier to weigh the amount of hay individually for each horse if you are to ensure that he receives the correct amount of bulk food for his size and work. The horse has to eat the hay as it comes and not by picking out the best first. It is important to make sure the haynet is tied at eye level, as if it is too low there is a risk that the horse may get his leg entangled in the net and injure himself, and if it is too high he will be uncomfortable and may get seed in his eyes, which can lead to eye trouble and is the reason for hay racks in stables being unpopular.

Oats as a food should be short, plump, clean, hard and dry. Oats are for energy and building up the body. They are often fed bruised or crushed to make them more easily digested. It is not normally advisable to feed oats to small ponies as oats are inclined to make them too hot and they become unmanageable.

Barley must be crushed or boiled until soft. It is a fattening food and more difficult than oats to digest. If introduced to the diet gradually, however, it can be a very valuable feed, particularly to old or thin horses.

Cubes, sometimes known as nuts, are a simple way of providing a balanced diet, although I personally feel that they become a rather monotonous way of keeping horses fed. Instructions on the packet should be read carefully as there are many different types, ranging from high-protein stud cubes to horse and pony cubes comprised mainly of a base of grass and vitamins. I believe they can be valuable to the diet if mixed with bran and carrots as a change to the normal feed plan. If you are feeding cubes, it is particularly important to remember to water the horse before feeding, as they occasionally mass together in the stomach.

Bran is the husk of wheat and for the types of feeding we are considering, the broader the bran the better it is. Bran adds bulk and salt to the diet and is obviously an essential constituent when making a bran mash. When fed wet it has a laxative effect, while dry bran has a binding effect, and is usefully fed to ponies at grass.

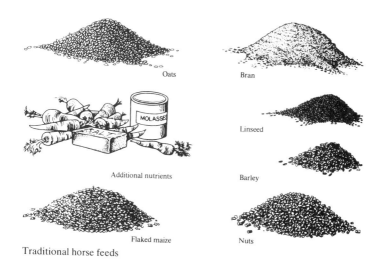

Oats

Bran

Linseed

Additional nutrients

Barley

Flaked maize

Nuts

Traditional horse feeds

Chaff, or chopped-up hay, adds bulk to the diet and may be used as well as, or instead of, bran to help the horse to masticate his food slowly. Chaff in the diet will often help slow down a horse who bolts his food.

Sugar beet is a popular bulk feed for ponies living out at grass in winter. It must be soaked overnight and be fed within forty-eight hours of soaking as it does not keep.

Linseed is a fattening food and excellent for getting the coat into good condition. It needs to be soaked for at least twelve hours and then boiled for about four hours before it can be fed. Weigh about 110g (¼lb) dry per horse. Quite often it is left to soak overnight and boiled fairly hard for about two hours. It is important to see that the seeds have burst, letting out not only the jelly but also the gases or acid, which are detrimental to the horse. Linseed in seed form is usually fed in a bran mash, which is made up in the following way. Take a bucket and about 1kg (2lb) of bran. Pour over it some water that is really boiling, and stir it with a spoon. Cover the bucket with a sack or cloth and allow the mash to steam for at least an hour. Before feeding, test to see that it is not too hot by plunging your hand into it. A bran mash is easily digested by a tired horse coming home after hunting or competing; the usual feed should be given about an hour and a half after the mash. Linseed can also be fed in oil form and a little added to the feed will act as an appetiser.

Unless you are an experienced horsemaster, it might be best, in the case of American readers only, to purchase a high quality 'mixed' or 'sweet' feed that includes a carefully planned and balanced combination of necessary grains. There are several good brands of mixed feeds available and labels should be carefully read for feeding instructions.

A generous guide to determine the correct quantity of food required is to allow, for a horse over 15 hands, between 12kg (27lb) and 14kg (32lb) of food a day in total, including hay, hard food and succulent additives. A pony under 15 hands will require 11kg (24lb) to 12.6kg (28lb) or less of food. Naturally the balance of hard and bulk feed will depend upon the temperament, age and type of work required of the animal, and should be conservatively determined as it can always be increased if necessary. For calculating the amount of hay to give a stabled horse, I allow 450g (1lb) hay for each hand in height, or for each 45kg (100lb) in weight. For example, a 12.2-hand pony will require approximately 6kg (13lb) of hay, whereas a 16-hand horse will require 7kg (16lb) of hay. There are, of course, exceptions to the rule, as certain horses tend to get too fat and must have their bulk reduced, while other animals seem never to put on as much weight as one would like and must be allowed to have as much hay as they wish to eat, but care must be taken not to overfeed.

Having established the amount of bulk feed necessary for your horse it is easy to decide upon the hard food. Take, for example, the 16-hand horse, receiving 7kg (16lb) of hay. In order to make his diet a total of 13.6kg (30lb) we have 6.3kg (14lb) available as hard food. A suitable diet for a working horse might be as follows:

1kg (2lb) oats four times a day
450g (1lb) bran four times a day
220g ($^1/_2$lb) cubes four times a day
110g ($^1/_4$lb) carrots twice a day
7kg (16lb) hay 2.7kg (6lb) in morning and 4.5kg (10lb) at night

6 Health, condition and exercise

The stabled horse will need regular exercise to keep him fit so he is able to do the work expected of him. There is a difference between 'exercise' and 'work' in that the horse is exercised in order that he will be in condition to do the work that is asked of him.

Initially you may be interested only in hacking, but as you become more experienced you may wish to hunt or show-jump. For this reason it is absolutely essential that the stable-kept horse receives regular exercise, in a way that is progressive without overtaxing him in any way. A horse is said to be in 'soft' condition when his muscles are slack, he has a large stomach and is carrying too much flesh without muscles and is therefore not capable of working without sweating or showing signs of distress. Horses that are turned out to grass in the summer and are not ridden, for example, are said to be in soft condition. A horse in 'hard' condition is physically capable of work without distress, his muscles will be firm, he will carry sufficient flesh to be in good health but no spare fat, his tendons will be hard and capable of sustained effort without injury.

It is important to understand the difference between soft and hard condition. A horse kept in a field who has a sleek summer coat and carries plenty of flesh, has a bright eye and a healthy outlook, is not necessarily in a fit physical state to work. This horse will have soft and flabby muscles and will not be capable of work without risk of strain to his heart, lungs and limbs. Fitness and good condition is the desirable physical state of the horse in work, and he must be allowed to develop the ability to do the work required of him without strain or stress. The kind of fitness may vary: a horse capable of fast work, such as racing or eventing, hunting or jumping, will be different in his fitness from one capable of slow, steady work for long periods — such as horses used for ploughing or riding-school work carrying beginners. To condition a horse for work it is important to achieve the correct balance between work and food.

Initially, the horse's work must be slow, and his diet will be mainly bulk food, that is to say hay. In addition to this he will need some succulents such as carrots, turnips, swedes and apples. His short feed will mainly consist of bran, and only a few oats: approximately 1 kg (2lb) a day. In the first week he should be given only half an hour of slow work each day progressing to three-quarters of an hour in the second week. In the third week introduce some work at the trot. As his work improves and becomes harder, so his food must also be gradually increased, by giving more concentrated and protein food such as oats and nuts, and less bulk food. The fitness programme will take a total of approximately eight weeks. Attention must be given to the horse's teeth, which may need to be rasped. He will also need to be wormed and to be shod. A stabled horse should be wormed at least four times a year and every six to eight weeks if turned out to grass. Use a powder or paste recommended by your vet.

It cannot be stressed too strongly that after any kind of exercise the horse must be allowed to cool off gradually before being given access to water or permitted to stand in a stall. Failure to do this properly may result in a colicky or sick horse.

Breaking out

There is a condition to be avoided known as 'breaking out': the horse, thoroughly dried when brought in from work, is later found in a cold sweat, usually on his neck and flanks and behind the ears. Try always to bring your horse home from exercise cool and calm. Walk on your feet the last half-mile, if necessary, to avoid work which may excite the horse, as breaking out is the result of a nervous state. Either the horse is worried by the work that he is doing, or by the rider's behaviour. If your horse has a tendency to break out, make sure he is thoroughly dry and warm when you arrive home, give him a haynet and then leave him alone. Check from time to time that he is all right.

Regular exercise is important for the horse's health and
condition, and work over ground rails helps to develop the
horse's muscles and promote fitness

A good bed of wood chips. The sides of the bed are banked up to ensure the
minimum of draughts and maximum comfort

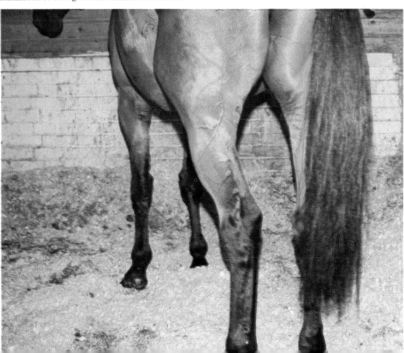

The loose-boxes. Notice that they are placed to receive the maximum amount of light and sun. The stable doors have two bolts for safety, one at the top of the half door and one at the bottom

The traditional form of bedding: a bed of wheat straw

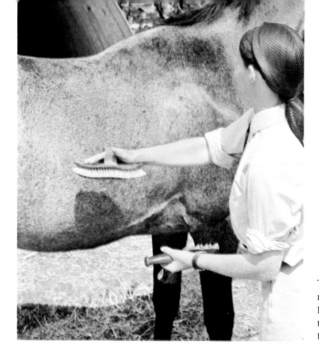

The complete grooming
routine should take half an
hour to forty minutes. Here
the groom is using the body
brush and curry comb

The body brush is also used to
groom the tail

Riding one horse and leading another is a simple way of exercising two horses at the same time. It is important that the led horse also wears a bridle

7 Roughing off and turning out to grass

A hunter who has worked a full season will have earned a thorough rest in the spring and early summer months in order to allow his system to relax and to enable him to grow big in condition again before the next hunting season. However, you cannot just turn a stabled horse into a field without any preparation. The process of letting down a horse before putting it out to grass is known as 'roughing off'.

First of all stop all strapping or complete grooming, using instead just a body brush, and gradually leaving off rugs. Let more air circulate around the horse's box. Cut out the corn feed gradually. As the hard feed is lessened so the amount of exercise that the horse receives may also be reduced. It is a good idea to turn the horse out into a well-fenced paddock for an hour or two during the warmest part of the day to begin with, so that in his diet he becomes more accustomed to grass instead of hard food.

If you wish to turn your horse out after the hunting season, you must first wait until his coat has really grown through. No horse should be turned out when his coat is clipped, except for a couple of hours in warm weather. Before finally turning him out, have his hind shoes removed, but leave the front ones on. Check that his teeth do not need rasping, and make sure he has been wormed. If the horse requires any other medication, this should also be done before he is finally turned out to grass. It is advisable if possible to wait until the spring grass is up if the horse is to derive the full benefit from his rest. Try to pick a dry spell, so that the grease in his coat is not washed out and he does not lose condition by becoming wet and cold. The best time to turn out a hunter is May until July. Add a supplementary small hard feed to the horse's diet if he is kept at grass during July and August, as the grass can then lose most of its nutrition value.

8   Care of the grass-kept horse

A suitably sized paddock for one horse or pony is approximately two acres; when keeping several horses in the same paddock, one and a half acres per horse will be enough. The fencing around a paddock must be sound, safe and adequate for the size of the animal in the field. A good height is 1.3m (4ft 6in). Ponies tend to push through hedges, wriggle under holes and escape, while horses may be inclined to jump over the top. A post and rail fence is the most suitable to use, but is unfortunately also the most expensive. A thick hedge with a ditch is also quite adequate.

Any form of fencing that contains a high proportion of wire should ideally be avoided, but if you must resort to using a wire fence (which *must not be* of barbed wire), it is essential that it is checked very regularly to ensure that the wire stays tightly strung. Wire injuries are often serious, since a horse could be permanently lamed from a tangle with the wire.

A good supply of fresh water is essential, available in a running stream or from a water trough. It goes without saying that the field must not have any holes, broken bottles or other rubbish around on which the horse could injure himself. Poisonous plants, such as deadly nightshade, yew, ragwort and ivy must be absent from the paddock as these plants could be literally deadly if eaten by a horse, so inspect your pasture regularly.

For the grass-kept horse, post and rail fences are best

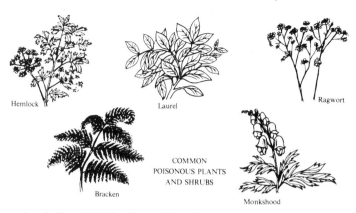

Hemlock

Laurel

Ragwort

Bracken

COMMON
POISONOUS PLANTS
AND SHRUBS

Monkshood

A windbreak in the form of a hedge, trees or a shelter is well worthwhile. In summer it provides protection from flies and sun; in winter the horse will appreciate some protection from the elements, and if he is to do well while at grass then a shelter is essential except for the hardiest types. Try to prevent mud from accumulating in the gateway or at the water trough, as it can become a great discomfort both to horses and humans if it freezes. Ideally, the gates ought to be situated on the highest part of the land, where good natural drainage is available. It is best not to have the gate and water trough too near to each other, as dangerous situations can arise when several horses are kept in a field together.

The spring and summer months are the most economical for keeping the horse at grass. Indeed, the horse that has been stabled throughout the winter period will enjoy an hour or two each day and benefit in health and condition, provided your grass is well cared for and in good supply, and your field within easy access from your stables. When selecting a field to keep your horse in try to buy, lease or rent one that is fairly close to your home, as although in the summer you may not mind visiting the field twice or three times daily, during short winter days a fair distance to travel may not be so convenient. What is available will of course depend on the locality in which you live; in suburban or town areas there may not be much choice. It must, however, be realized that a horse cannot live on a dried out, discarded, or horse-sick pasture. The paddock must be well-maintained and contain many good grasses, few inferior ones and no poisonous plants.

In a field with good pasture it should not be necessary to feed your horse any hay at all by springtime, if he is doing no work. If, however, the horse is required to work for one or two hours every day, with perhaps a little competitive work as well, then he will need a supplementary feed of oats, bran and horse and pony cubes. Visit your horse first thing in the morning, check him over for cuts and injuries, make sure that his water supply is fresh and working properly, that the fencing is still sound, catch the horse and go over his body, mane and tail area lightly with a little fly spray, and then give him his short feed.

On the days that you are riding him you may prefer to catch the horse in the morning and feed him on returning to the stable after exercise. If, however, you do not own a stable, then it is perfectly all right to feed him in the field. You must remember, however, that it would be harmful to the horse to work him on a full stomach, and he must have an hour's rest after a feed before being ridden, to allow him to digest his food properly and to avoid the risk of colic. The horse may be turned out in his field after his early morning feed or kept up and ridden and turned out after his exercise. It should not be necessary for him to be inspected again during the day but he must be looked at again in the evening.

During the autumn and winter months there is little grass in the fields and certainly the feed value is poor, so your horse will need both hay and short feeds. The hay gives the bulk to the diet, making the horse feel full when he will no longer be able to get sufficient grass, and the short feeds will give the necessary protein and vitamins for his health, fitness and condition. At this time of the year the horse will also need food to keep him warm. Another way to help keep the horse warm is to put a New Zealand rug on him. This is a waterproof sheet, lined with wool, which keeps the rain off the horse's back and helps keep him warm. It is important to look at the water during the winter, as it may have become frozen and need to have the ice broken. The gateway will probably become very poached so do not feed him there.

For a grooming programme, see page 26.

9 Bringing up after rest at grass and conditioning

If the horse is required for hunting he must be brought up from grass at the end of July or the beginning of August. It will take a period of six to eight weeks to get the animal in hard condition again after his rest period. If you have followed the earlier advice when the horse was at grass and have fed a small hard feed daily through the month of July then the change in diet for your horse when he first comes in will not be too difficult for his digestive system to adjust to. However, there are various problems that can arise if the horse does not receive the very best of care and attention in the first few days when in from grass. Horses just up from grass are prone to filled legs and humour spots.

The following procedures may help to prevent this happening to your horse. All hard food must be introduced and increased gradually; filled legs and humour spots are caused primarily by over-feeding. The corn ration must be increased slowly according to the exercise that the horse is receiving. All feeds should be damp, including the hay. A properly cooked bran or linseed mash is a valuable adjunct to the diet. In the first few days the horse will be liable to suffer from a cough, a cold or a sore throat. To guard against these ensure that he has plenty of fresh air, always leaving open the top half of the stable door. The damping of all feeds helps to avoid coughs. The horse must receive only light exercise in the first week so that there is no risk of his sweating. An unfit horse is also prone to a sore back and girth galls, and from the very first day in the stable I thoroughly recommend that the back, saddle, girth and bit areas should be dressed with a strong saline solution to help harden them and thus guard against sores. A numnah will also help to prevent soreness on the back. It is possible that the horse's usual saddle will not fit when he first comes in from grass; make sure you check that it does not pinch him. It can be a good idea to work the horse slowly on the lunge for the first few days to get him a little hardened before being ridden.

The most important rule to remember when bringing the horse in is that all work must be taken slowly at first. After a week of daily half-hour walking and another of three-quarters of an hour, I usually introduce a little road work to strengthen the tendons, and towards the end of the third week begin to trot for short periods. In the fourth and fifth weeks I continue along these lines, gradually introducing a little hill work to improve the wind and strengthen the back by making the horse use his shoulders and balance himself. If all has been going well in the sixth week I begin some work at the canter, progressing with more trot and walking exercises so that my horse is capable of an hour and a half of exercise. During this time I would have been reducing the quantities of bulk food and increasing the concentrates, so that by the seventh and eighth weeks the horse should be capable of two hours' exercise, including some canter work, without undue strain.

The procedure that is outlined above applies to any horse that has had a long period of rest at grass. The golden rule is that any fitness programme must be slow and gradual, with the horsemaster carefully inspecting the horse daily, noticing the colour of the membrane of the eye, the softness and colour of the coat, the state of the droppings and the urine, the appetite, the amount of water taken, and gaining an impression of the horse's personal pattern of behaviour. Any sudden change in this behaviour pattern should be noticed immediately, and be respected as just cause for worry. The horse must be given the opportunity and the time to tone up his muscles and this can only be done if the ratio of food to exercise and work is suited to the needs of the individual horse.

10   Shoeing

Everyone interested in good stable management should have an understanding of the art of shoeing. As a general rule the foot should receive attention at least once a month; otherwise it may become too long, the horse will begin to stumble and the toe will turn up. Something like one-ninth of the foot should be rasped off every six weeks; the hoof will take nine to fifteen months to grow from top to bottom. It is important to test the horse for lameness before a visit to or by the farrier, and again after the horse has been shod.

The iron from which shoes are made is bought by the bar, which may be concave and fullered. The farrier fashions the shape and stamps holes in the shoe at an angle to the toe, usually three or four to the outside and three inside. He should try always to use as few nails (clenches) as possible to secure the shoe.

The actual shoeing operation begins with the removal of the old shoe. The clenches are raised with the buffer and hammer, and the shoe is then pulled off with pincers. It is best to start on the inside edge at the heel, and to ease the shoe off firmly by using the pincers on either side at the heel, working towards the toe. When the shoe is removed the hoof should be taken down with a rasp. It is advisable not to use a knife or pincers for this operation unless there is excessive growth.

The frog should never be rasped or cut, except to remove diseased parts or old tissue. The bars of the feet should not be interfered with either, as the horse may develop contracted heels if they are cut. When the horse is shod hot (that is, the shoe is heated before being shaped to the foot), the foot should just be scorched to see that it is even. The outside wall of the foot should not be rasped except to make a nick for the nail to fit in. It is also a good idea to cut a small piece at the toe so that the toe clip will lie snugly into the foot without needing to be hammered back. Nailing on the shoe is, of course, a job for the farrier. A misplaced nail will cause considerable pain and possibly permanent damage. The nail must go between the outer edge and the white line; if it is too near the white line, pressure will be formed and cause nail binding, or a prick if right inside. The nail should come out approximately 3.8cm ($1^1/_2$in) up the hoof, and the end is twisted off and turned over neatly to form a clench.

Dumping is a term used to describe the action of cutting back the toe to make the foot fit the shoe, rather than the shoe fitting the foot. Dumping exposes the horny wall to the extent that it becomes brittle, and eventually it becomes impossible to put a nail into it.

An experienced farrier can do a lot from a surgical point of view to lessen defects in action and conformation, and also to assist in a cure of some ailments by variation from the normal shoeing methods. It must be remembered that when surgical shoeing is employed a programme of appropriate exercise must be considered and carefully arranged. If surgical shoeing is considered necessary, follow the advice of your vet and the farrier, who will usually work together to achieve what is required.

Studs

Studs are used to give a horse confidence when jumping, enabling him to jump and gallop on all types of going. If the going is heavy the horse's shoes should be fitted with screw holes all round, and large square-shaped studs can be used. In circumstances where the going may have been rather hard but then a shower of rain makes it very slippery, it may be best to use pointed studs in all four feet. If the ground is perfect, with a little spring in it, I would recommend the use of small studs all round for dressage, large dome-shaped ones for show-jumping, and large pointed studs in the hind feet only for cross-country work. I prefer to limit the use of studs for cross-country work because in a fall there is less chance of the rider being hurt by a blow from a hindleg than from foreleg. When competing, make sure your horse is freshly shod so

Using the stud 'tap' to clean out the hole that is to receive the stud

Removing the oiled cotton wool from the screw-hole in preparation for the stud

When the horse has finished work, the stud must be removed
and replaced by cotton-wool

Pulling on an overreach boot

Pulling the mane to thin and shorten it is best done by twisting the hair around a mane comb

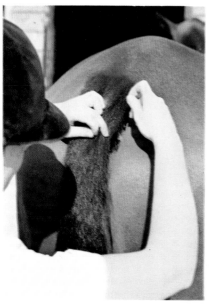

Trimming the tail by hand. This should be done after exercise or on a warm day when the pores are open

Canter work is essential as part of your fitness programme to
strengthen the horse's stomach muscles

A plain snaffle bridle with cavesson noseband suitable for a pony

the screw threads are not worn. Clean out the stud holes the night before the competition with a nail and your stud 'tap'. Plug the clean holes with cotton-wool soaked in oil, and you will find that the studs will go in easily and without panic on the day of the competition.

When you have finished competing, remove the studs with a spanner and plug the holes with oily cotton-wool again, to prevent their becoming filled with dirt. Naturally, you must not travel your horse with his studs in, as the risk of injury is too great. It would be only too easy for the horse to lose his balance in the box or trailer and severely injure himself with his own feet.

Here the farrier is in the process of fitting the heated shoe to the foot

11 Clipping and trimming

Considerable emphasis has been given to the importance of cleaning a horse. One reason for this is that it helps to keep the animal in condition during the winter months. A heavy coat has the same effect on a horse as a Turkish bath does on a human being, or the working of a horse in heavy rugs. It will make him sweat and he may even begin to lose condition. An animal with a short coat dries easily, and is therefore less liable to chills and is easier to keep clean. After a horse has been clipped nature provides a layer of fat underneath the skin as protection against the cold, and the warmth of a heavy winter coat can be replaced by rugs. A horse with a heavy coat is not capable of strenuous work without at least some distress being caused. The more a horse is clipped the easier it is to keep him in condition. The best time of the year to clip is when the winter coat has set, normally in October, and then every two or three weeks after that until January. It is preferable not to clip after January, as late clipping may hinder the growth of the summer coat and spoil the good-looking coat that would be required for summer shows.

There are four main types of clip: hunter clip, full clip, trace clip and blanket clip.

A hunter clip is a special technique as hunters normally have their legs left unclipped as protection against chills, thorns, mud, fever and cracked heels. The saddle patch sometimes is left, although a decision on that depends very much upon the coarseness of the coat. A horse with a thick winter coat is best clipped right out the first time and the saddle patch left on the second time. This protects the skin under the saddle, which is otherwise liable to injury and soreness after a long day's hunting.

With a full clip, the horse is clipped all over. For horses with a heavy coat it becomes much easier to dry the legs and back, but very special attention must be given to providing adequate warmth to avoid the risk of his catching chills.

In giving a trace clip, the coat is removed below the trace line, that is, on the lower part of the chest, the belly, flanks and quarters. The legs are left. This is a particularly useful clip for ponies or horses hunted off grass, who can be turned out in a New Zealand rug — a particularly warm kind of rug which is waterproof and has leg straps to keep it secure.

For a blanket clip, the coat is removed from the neck and shoulders following a line similar to that of the trace clip.

There are points at which clippers should not be used. The ears should never be clipped on the inside, but just down to level with the lobes. Great care must be taken never to allow clipped hair to fall inside the ear, since infection may easily develop. The inside hair is a natural protection from cold and a filter against dust and dirt. The heels and fetlocks can be trimmed either with small clippers or with scissors and comb.

It is essential that the clippers used are clean and well oiled, and experience suggests that the best means of doing this is to clean the blades with kerosene after use, and to dry them carefully to prevent rust. The blade tension must be tight enough to clip, but not so tight that the blades become warped with the heat of the machine. Frequent brushing clean, followed by oiling during a clipping session will improve the clippers' performance and retard the heat build-up. It goes without saying that the plug must be well earthed to prevent shock, and that the leads should be long enough to allow movement in the stable when clipping, and to be safely arranged so that the horse cannot step on the cable.

There are points to remember when preparing to clip. For example, the horse must be well strapped, and standing on a dry surface. Dirt should be removed as it will quickly blunt the blades, pull the hair and make the horse restless. It is important that the stable is well lit if a good job is to be achieved.

The clippers must not be pushed or forced; the weight of the head of the clippers alone is sufficient to clip well. Clip against the lie of the hair, beginning on the neck and taking as much as possible in one sweep. I usually begin where it is least noticeable but where the horse is not too sensitive, so I can adjust the tension correctly to remove the coat as neatly as possible. It is often wise to allow the clippers to run for a minute or two before clipping in order to accustom the horse to the noise.

Until you have some experience in clipping I suggest that you mark with chalk or soap both the leg and the saddle patch (by putting a saddle on the horse and marking round it) before beginning to clip. Be as quiet as you can and ask someone to help you to reassure the horse and hold him still. Give the horse a small net of hay to pick out so that he is otherwise occupied. Leave the head until last, just in case it makes the horse nervous. A 'twitch' is sometimes used when clipping the head of a nervous horse, but is not recommended. This device consists of a handle with a rope loop at one end that holds the horse's upper lip and keeps him still. Its misuse can cause severe restriction to the circulation and may make the horse head shy in the future.

A clipped horse will require clothing to replace the winter coat. A jute rug (see page 57) with one or two woollen under-blankets is generally sufficient, but individual horses vary and careful observation is necessary.

Trimming

Careful trimming will improve the appearance of every type of horse, and is practised by all good grooms. The hairs of the mane and tail will pluck more easily when the pores of the skin and warm and open, that is, after exercise or on a warm day. Some horses will fidget and pain may be caused if pulling is done in very cold weather when the pores of the skin are closed. The mane is normally pulled to thin out an over-thick mane, to reduce a long mane to the required length, or to permit the mane to lie flat. The longest hairs form underneath, and these should be dealt with first and removed a few at a time by winding them around the finger or by using a pulling comb. The whole operation need not necessarily be completed in one session, which may make the horse's crest sore — something he will remember when you next try to pull his mane! Never pull the top hairs, nor any that may stand up after

54

Tail pulling with a comb

plaiting, because they will form an upright fringe on the crest. On no account must scissors or clippers be used on the mane. A tail is pulled to improve its shape and appearance and to show off the hindquarters. Tail pulling is also done by plucking out the hairs, beginning at the top of the tail and underneath, and working all the way down until a good shape is achieved. Pull only a few hairs at a time. Some people feel that the end of the tail looks neatest if it is 'banged', that is, cut straight across with scissors at a level about 10cm (4in) below the point of the hock. It will then be on a line with the hock when carried in movement. Clipping, trimming and the pulling of the mane and the tail are best done under the supervision of an expert at first.

Plaiting

The object of plaiting a mane is to show off the neck and head of the horse. If they are naturally good-looking, small, tight plaits will further enhance them. If your horse's neck is straight and lacking in crest, or tends to be ewe-necked, you can improve his appearance by clever plaiting. The mane can be plaited to give the illusion of more breadth if you brush it over to the near side and spray the top hair halfway down with lacquer, then brush over to the off side, plait and roll into neat knobs. The number of plaits will depend on the length of your horse's neck and the thickness of his mane. A short-necked horse will look better with a lot of plaits, whereas a long-necked horse will seem to be more correctly proportioned if he has fewer plaits.

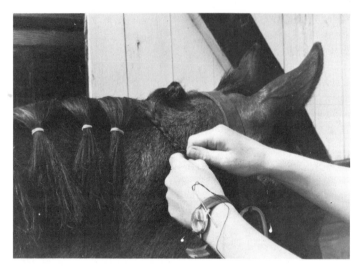

Plaiting the mane will improve the appearance of the horse's head and neck for the show ring. The plait is finished off by fastening the end with a needle and thread

12   Clothing

It is impossible to overstress the importance of ensuring that the horse's rugs, blankets, bandages and boots are at all times kept scrupulously clean if skin trouble is to be avoided. In addition, the leather work found in buckles to fasten the fronts of rugs, boot straps and rollers, should be kept supple with the use of a good brand of saddle soap or neats-foot oil, and petroleum jelly for storage through the summer.

The most important and commonly used piece of stable clothing is the jute rug, primarily intended to keep the horse warm in winter. This is shaped to fit the horse and is measured in lengths from the wither to the top of the horse's tail. As an example, a horse standing at 15.2 hands might require a rug that is 1.8m (5ft 9in) long, depending on the length of his back. A jute rug is made of hessian or hemp and is a very hardwearing material. It often has a woollen lining.

In winter a stable-kept horse who has been clipped will require one or two lightweight under-blankets in addition to his rug. These are merely square under-rugs that may be purchased from army-surplus stores and saddlery shops. The army rugs are usually reasonably inexpensive, and are quite adequate for the purpose of keeping the horse warm when his natural coat has been removed. As an ordinary rug will not have the attached surcingles of a fitted one, a separate roller surcingle will be necessary. When the stable rug is fitted, care must be taken to ensure that neither the rug nor the under-blanket presses down on the withers or the spine of the horse, as any tightness in these areas may cause a sore back or wither.

Use the following procedure when rugging up. Hold the left side of the rug towards the front, in your left hand, and the right side gathered up in your right hand. Approach the horse on the nearside shoulder, and speak quietly to him so that he is not nervous. Gently throw the rug over his neck, pull it back to the correct position, smooth it so that there are no wrinkles, attach the roller, and finally buckle the front of the rug itself. In this way the wool side will be next to the horse and the canvas or material on the outside.

To remove the rug, unfasten the buckle at the front, remove the roller, and place it in a corner of the box. Next, with both hands, take the front half of the rug and fold it back over the back portion, then, with the left hand in the centre-front and the right hand in the middle of the back portion, remove the rug and under-blanket together in one gentle sweep in the direction of the lay of the horse's coat. Shake out the rug to air, and fold it away until it is required to go back on to the horse again.

A wool rug of a similar shape and design is often used for warmth when travelling, or wherever the horse needs to be smart at shows, and is frequently edged in a bright colour contrasting with that of the rug itself. It is a popular habit to have a monogram embroidered on the rug for appearance and recognition. In the summer it is usually safe to remove the rugs totally in warm weather, but if the nights are on the cold side a lightweight rug made of cotton or linen may be used. This type of covering is called a cotton sheet, summer sheet or fly sheet, so named because it is used for travelling to shows in the summer to prevent the horse being worried by flies, and at the same time to keep his coat clean and free from dust. If a horse should return home wet and cold, it is a good idea to put a jute rug on him, inside out, and pad it with straw underneath. This absorbs the moisture and creates ventilation, which helps the horse to dry more quickly.

Another style of rug often used on horses that are either hot, or cold and wet, is the anti-sweat rug or 'cooler', which works on the same principle as that of a man's string vest. It is full of holes and allows good ventilation while trapping a layer of warm air. Used in conjunction with a sheet, which should be laid on top, it enables the horse to cool down slowly and yet dry quickly, which helps to prevent the horse from catching a chill.

A woollen day rug, used for warmth and appearance

A cotton sheet keeps the horse's coat clean in summer

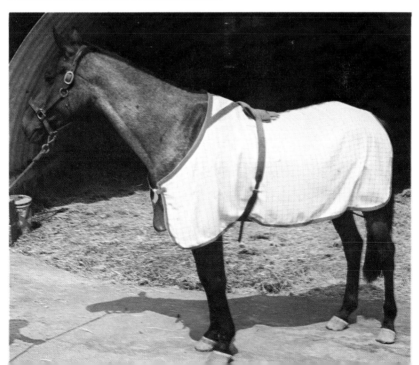

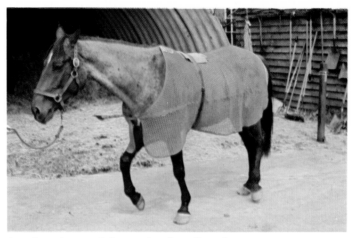

An anti-sweat rug, used after exercise, often with another rug on top. This helps the horse to cool off and dry without catching a chill

A well-fitting dressage saddle. Notice the low girth attachment and the deep central seat

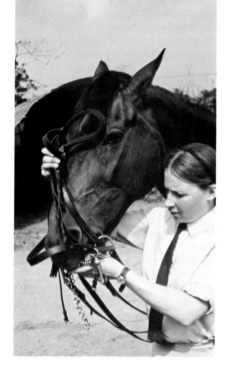

Fitting a double bridle. The
left hand holds the two bits,
while the fingers encourage
the horse to open his mouth

Once the bits are in the
mouth, the forelock is pulled
over the browband

61

The double bridle, finally fitted to perfection

13 Bandaging

Bandaging a horse should be carried out only by experts, as tremendous harm can be done to the limbs of a horse if a bandage is poorly applied. It is worth practising, however, (on your *own* legs, at first) until you are really capable of doing the job properly. Here are some general guidelines to help you. Never draw one part of the bandage tighter than another, as this will apply an unequal pressure to the limb. The tapes must not be tighter than the rest of the bandage, as this could cause a swelling. Tapes are best tied on the outside of the leg, not on the inside of the leg or on the front or back tendons. I find it preferable to bandage with cotton-wool or gamgee underneath the bandage to ensure that there is even pressure all the way down the leg.

The stable bandage is normally 2–3m (7–8ft) long and about 12cm (5in) wide; it is made of wool, flannel or stockinette. The purpose of the stable bandage is to give warmth and protection to the limb and to encourage good circulation. It can also be used for protection and warmth when travelling. Properly fitted, the stable bandage should begin just below the knee and continue down over the fetlock joint to the horse's heel. To make a good job of fitting, first leave a 'V'-shaped endpiece pointing to the rear; bandage once round the limb and fold down the endpiece. Continue bandaging by winding the material round the leg, each turn passing two-thirds of the way down the previous turn's width of bandage. Work all the way down the leg and then back to the middle, finally tying the tapes on the outside and tucking the loose ends underneath. It should be comfortably snug but not tight.

Exercise bandages require even greater skill than stable bandages in their application. The exercise bandage is usually about 1.5m (5ft) long and 10cm (4in) wide, made of crêpe or stockinette. It is definitely advisable to use gamgee beneath an exercise bandage to ensure equal pressure — cotton-wool will serve almost as well. Exercise bandages give support, particularly to the horse's back tendons and suspensory ligament. Their use is recommended because when jumping a horse usually lands first on one leg only, and this sudden jar can cause a sprain. The exercise bandage should extend from just below the knee to above the fetlock joint. It must be sewn in position on every occasion, since tapes could break or come undone and cause an accident. A little gamgee should be visible at the top and bottom of the bandage, which should be applied firmly and evenly without wrinkles. If the going is heavy, an elastic bandage 7.5cm (3in) wide is very handy and neat to use in giving adequate support. The ends should still be sewn, even with an adhesive elastic bandage.

Cold-water bandages are applied to help remove heat from the legs. A stockinette bandage is the best type to use. Place it in cold water before applying it to the leg and change it every twenty minutes. Alternatively, one can hose the bandage for five minutes every fifteen minutes or so. The disadvantage of this method is that the bandage tends to take up the heat of the leg, and I find it preferable to hose the leg itself. Either stand the horse in a stream of running water, or hose the leg for thirty minutes twice or three

| The stable bandage. Notice how the gamgee covers the heel | The stable bandage is secured with a bow that is simple to untie | The finished bandage. The ends of the tapes are neatly tucked into the bandage |

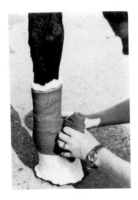

The tail bandage. Here you
see the first stage: notice the
end in the groom's hand

The end of the tail bandage is
folded over the first loop and
then wound round

The finished tail bandage

times a day. Too much hosing can, however, cause chafed heels,
and it is advisable to grease the heels with Vaseline before hosing
so that the water does not penetrate them.

Tail bandages are made of crêpe or elastic and are used to
protect the tail when travelling and to improve the appearance of a
'pulled' tail. A tail bandage should be firmly but not too tightly
fitted, starting at the top of the dock. Unroll the bandage closely
down the tail until the end of the dock and then return about half
the way up. The tail bandage should be tied in the same way as a
stable bandage, care being taken to ensure that the tapes are looser
than the bandage so that circulation is not impaired in any way. A
tail bandage should not be left on for longer than six hours. To
remove the tail bandage, stand behind the horse a little to one side
so as to avoid any risk of injury, and with both hands clasp the tail
and bandage at the top of the dock. Pull the tail bandage gently
down the tail so as not to disturb the lay of the hair.

To roll up a stable or tail bandage, fold the tapes neatly into the
top end of the bandage and roll the tapes and bandage together
firmly, using both hands and a knee roll and keeping the bandage
flat to avoid wrinkles. (The tapes must be on the inside so they are
on the outside when the bandage is put on!)

14 Saddlery: its fitting, care and maintenance

The correct fitting of both saddles and bridles is important to the comfort and performance of the horse. The saddle must be neither too big nor too small. If it is over-sized it may press on the loins and damage the kidneys, or it may ride up on the horse's neck; if it is too small it may pinch the horse. The weight of the saddle should be taken on either side of the spine, not on the spine itself or the horse's withers, and for this reason the front arch or pommel must not be too low — or too narrow, as it could again pinch the withers.

Further important guidelines when fitting a saddle are as follows. There should be a clear channel along the spine of the horse; from behind you should be able to see daylight along the saddle, with no pressure along the spine at any point. The saddle must be centrally balanced, with a deep seat to encourage the rider to sit in the correct position, which will encumber the horse as little as possible. When fitting a new saddle on a horse it is important that the rider sits in the saddle to see whether there is any pressure. The styles of saddles vary considerably, so make sure you buy one of a suitable type. If possible, arrange to ride in a saddle before you decide to purchase it. An all-purpose springtree saddle is the best all-round type and is suitable for most activities.

How to saddle-up and unsaddle

On entering the stable put a headcollar on your horse and tie him up. Next remove the rugs, and by approaching on the near side, put the saddle gently onto the horse's back. If you put the saddle too far forward and then slide it back into the correct position, you will know that the hairs are lying smooth underneath. Next, attach the girth loosely, and pull the buckle guards over the buckles of the girth. Then pull each foreleg forward to ensure that no skin is pinched and the hair is lying flat and comfortable. The stirrups should not be let down until the horse is outside the stable, when the girth may also be tightened.

Before removing a saddle after exercise, it is best to let out the girth by a hole for the last half-mile to allow the blood to circulate thoroughly through the back. On returning home, dismount, run the stirrups up the leathers so there is no risk of injury to the horse, and then enter the stable. In the stable, undo the girth on the near side, go round the off side and buckle the girth to the girth straps, or fold it through the stirrup iron, so that it does not hang loose and bump against the horse. Return to the near side and lift off the saddle. Massage the back for a few minutes and then put the saddle away safely on a saddle rack.

The cleaning of saddlery

First place your saddle on a saddle horse, and then collect together your cleaning equipment. You will need a bucket of warm water, saddle soap, two sponges, a chamois leather, metal polish and rags.

Remove the girth, stirrup leathers and irons from the saddle and also the buckle guards. Thoroughly clean the saddle by washing with warm water, using a sponge or cloth. Dry the saddle with a chamois leather which has been wrung out in the water. Next, with the second sponge soap all the leather work on the saddle very liberally, rubbing it well in to keep the leather supple and soft. The metal work — buckles, rings, and stirrup irons — should be washed if very dirty, and then polished with metal polish and rubbed with a clean rag to give a good shine. The saddle should ideally be put away on a specially made peg or bracket, though it can rest on the saddle horse until required.

The equipment needed for cleaning a bridle is the same as that of the saddle. In addition, however, a hook hanging from the ceiling is very helpful. Take the bridle to pieces, putting each piece safely on a table; wash, dry, and soap each part separately. Wash, dry and polish the bit, but if you use metal polish on the mouth piece wash it again in hot water so that there are no traces of metal polish left on the bit. The bit is going in the horse's mouth, and polish tastes very unpleasant. After the bridle has been cleaned put it together again and hang it on the cleaning hook, and then go over all the leather work again with the saddle-soap sponge, being careful to keep the sponge well soaped but as dry as possible. A wet sponge will cause a lather of soap, which is very messy. As a matter of course, when you are cleaning tack you should check that the stitching and leather work is all in good repair. Any weaknesses should be repaired immediately, as weak, faulty saddlery could cause a bad accident.

Saddle linings

Having talked about the saddle I will deal with linings for saddles. There are three main types: leather, linen and serge. Leather is the best, and by far the most common, because it is long-lasting and keeps the cleanest. The linings must be well looked after by washing and saddle soaping after use, or the leather will crack and become hard, giving the horse a sore back. A linen lining, like serge, has to be replaced more often than leather. To care for linen linings, scrub them with soap and water and leave them to dry naturally. Serge is more difficult to keep clean and is best sponged with warm water and brushed with a stiff brush when dry.

Bits

These are pieces of metal, rubber, vulcanite or nylon or similar material which is placed in the horse's mouth and held in position by the bridle. The reins are attached to rings on the bit through which the rider communicates with the horse. It is by having a bit (in conjunction with the use of feet and legs) that the rider is able to control, guide and demand obedience and precise movements.

There are three main types of bit: the snaffle, pelham and curb. The snaffle can be jointed, double-jointed, straight bar or mullen mouth. The most common jointed bit is the eggbutt snaffle, which has a fixed ring so that no pinching occurs. It has a nutcracker action on the tongue and acts on the lips and corners of the mouth.

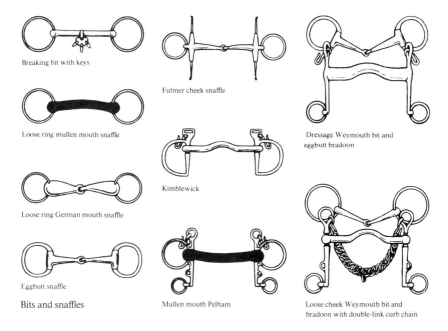

Breaking bit with keys

Loose ring mullen mouth snaffle

Loose ring German mouth snaffle

Eggbutt snaffle

Bits and snaffles

Fulmer cheek snaffle

Kimblewick

Mullen mouth Pelham

Dressage Weymouth bit and
eggbutt bradoon

Loose cheek Weymouth bit and
bradoon with double-link curb chain

The mullen mouth snaffle is a slightly curved bit and presses only mildly on the tongue and corners of the mouth. A rubber snaffle is by its very composition light, soft and therefore a mild bit; it is often used on young horses or on horses with fussy mouths.

The double-jointed bit has a nutcracker action on the tongue, but presses on top of the tongue and causes a pinching action. It also acts on the lips and corners of the mouth.

If you need to discover which kind of bit best suits your horse, begin with the mildest type, the rubber snaffle, or perhaps a hollow-mouth German snaffle which is made of metal, is fairly thick, and has only one joint. (The thicker the bit the milder it will be.) The jointed snaffle comes next; there are many types, the eggbutt, already described, is the most common. Twisted wire snaffles are one of the most severe of any bits, and should be used with great care. Then would come the straight bar and finally the double-jointed snaffle.

69

The pelham is a slightly more severe bit. It is a combination of the snaffle and the curb. There are several types, most of them with a very similar snaffle action. They act on the tongue and on the bars of the mouth with a leverage effect which encourages the horse to flex at the poll. The most popular type of pelham is the Kimblewick, a very mild pelham with little leverage. It is good for strong children's ponies, though some ponies and horses will not accept it and do not 'go' in it well, disliking the tongue groove. If a stronger bit than a snaffle is needed a half-moon pelham may prove more satisfactory. This has a mullen mouthpiece which is slightly curved, with a cheek (shank) on either side where both a snaffle and a curb rein may be fixed. This bit tries to have the same effect as the double bridle with only one mouthpiece; as a compromise it is quite successful, but it does not have the precision of a double bridle. Other bits in the pelham range are the Scamperdale and the jointed pelham.

The curb bit is the most severe of the three classes of bits. The curb may be combined with a small snaffle bit known as a bradoon, the combination being known as the double bridle. The curb has great leverage on the poll, encouraging the horse to flex. Like the pelham it acts on the tongue and the bars of the mouth; the 'fulcrum' is the curb chain which acts in the chin groove. In skilled hands the double is a delicate aid, allowing the rider to achieve maximum precision and control. The double bridle is used for dressage at medium and advanced level, for showing and

Curb chains

70

traditionally for hunting, although in the United States the latter two sports are increasingly using variations of the snaffle. The double bridle should not, however, be used on the young horse until he is going really well in a simple snaffle bit, nor should an inexperienced rider attempt to use it.

All bits must be fitted correctly and always sensibly. By this I mean that it is not a compliment to one's horsemanship to put a horse in a severe bit or use a lot of gadgets; such aids should only be used when absolutely necessary. All bits when fitted should just wrinkle the corners of the lips and be wide enough so as not to pinch the corners of the mouth, but not so wide as to protrude more than 1cm ($^1/_2$in or so) when held straight in the horse's mouth.

Other artificial aids

A martingale is a device which helps to regulate the head carriage of a horse. The running martingale, which is the only kind allowed in show-jumping events, acts by pressure on the mouth. The martingale must have stops fitted on the reins to prevent its rings becoming hooked on the buckle of the rein near the bit. When fitting the running martingale it is best to attach it to the reins and then, by gentle pressure on the rein, fit the martingale so that it comes into operation only when the horse raises his head too high above an angle of control.

The standing martingale runs from the girth to the noseband,

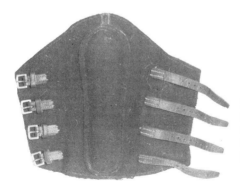

The inside of the brushing boot. Used to protect the forelock joint, they are most important when lungeing the horse

71

and acts by pressure on the nose to prevent the head coming up above the level of the withers. This type of martingale must never be used with a drop noseband (see below).

An Irish martingale is simply a loop of leather through which the reins pass, and it is carried under the neck. It is normally used on young racehorses, as it prevents the reins being thrown over the head of the horse. There are usually two rings attached by a piece of double-sewn leather 11cm (4^1/$_2$in) long.

Running reins are attached from the girth or saddle through the rings of the bit and to the rider's hand, serving as an artificial aid in keeping the horse's head down. It is best to use them together with an ordinary rein, they should be used only for schooling, and by an experienced rider for hunting or jumping.

A drop noseband is useful as it helps to prevent a horse opening his mouth and therefore improves control. It fits below the bit and in the chin groove and above the nostrils. In no way should it interfere with the horse's breathing.

A grackle is a figure-of-eight noseband, which combines the action of a drop noseband and a cavesson while allowing the use of a martingale.

The various boots designed for the horse to wear serve to protect the legs from injury when jumping cross-country fences, show-jumping, or schooling, and particularly when lungeing. There are several types of boot in general use. Tendon boots are used in front and behind and give protection to the leg, particularly of the horse that is working at speed. The skeleton kneecap is a boot shaped to the front of the knee, and is used to protect young horses when schooling over solid timber. Lightweight brushing boots are made of leather, kersey or vinyl to protect the fetlock joint and cannon bone. An over-reach boot is a useful device for horses that are jumping big fences and therefore may land unbalanced and strike their foreleg at the heel with their hind leg. This boot is usually made of rubber and fits closely to the heel. Bell-shaped, it covers the lower portion of the pastern bone and hoof.

Travelling kneecaps, as their name implies, are used to protect the knees when travelling, and are also useful for road exercise.

Above: over-reach boots are essential for jumping. The rubber over-reach boots on the forelegs are used to protect the horse's heel

Knee caps are used to protect the knee while travelling or on road exercise. The top strap is fastened, while the bottom one is loose to allow flexion to the knee

15   Care of the horse's teeth

The horse's teeth should be examined for sharp edges every three months. The edges of the molar teeth in both the upper and lower row will become sharp with wear and may possibly cause injuries to the tongue and cheeks. If the teeth are sharp the horse will be unable to masticate his food properly and will not gain full benefit from his diet. It is an easy task, although a tiring one, for your veterinary surgeon to rasp the teeth. It is reasonably simple to determine whether your horse's teeth need to be rasped by holding his tongue with one hand, so he cannot bite you by mistake, and with your free hand to feel the molar teeth with your fingers. If they appear rough then without doubt they need attention. In some instances the outer edge of the molar teeth can be felt from the outside of the jaw near the cheek-bone, and if these seem rough and unbalanced, then again you can be fairly sure that rasping is required. It is a mistake to think that only old horses need to have their teeth rasped; many young horses have teeth which become sharp and need expert attention.

Wolf teeth are often developed when the horse is only six months old, and as they have very little root they are liable to erupt and disappear at the same time as the milk teeth behind them. If the wolf teeth are not shed, it is best to have your veterinary surgeon remove them as they can interfere with the horse's ability to bite in later life, and can cause him much discomfort.

Types of teeth

1 Molars or grinding teeth, twelve in each jaw.
2 Incisors or biting teeth, six in each jaw.
3 Tusks (tushes) or canine teeth, two in each jaw.
4 Wolf teeth — occasionally occur in upper jaw just in front of

the molars; should be removed if they interfere with the bit

Of the molars, the first three on each side are only temporary. There are two types of incisor: the temporary, milk or foal teeth which are whitish and small; and the permanent, which are yellowish in colour. The central teeth appear first, the lateral teeth second, and the corner teeth later.

Ageing by the teeth

Although a horse's teeth are our most accurate guide to its age, it must be realized that there will be some slight variation from horse to horse. At birth a foal has no teeth, but after about ten days two centrals appear in the top and bottom jaw. At two months the laterals appear. These are fully in wear at one year, but the corner teeth are shelly, that is, with only a little wear on top. At two years all are in full wear. At two years and three months the horse should show signs of permanent teeth coming by a redness of the gums. At two years and six months the permanent centrals appear. At three years the permanent centrals are in wear. When the horse is three years and six months the permanent laterals appear, and they are in wear at four years and six months. At approximately four and a half years the corner teeth appear, and when the horse is five years all the teeth are grown through, although the corners will not be in full wear. A horse at this age is said to have a 'full mouth'. When the horse is between four and five years old he will grow his tusk (this only applies to geldings and entires, not mares). The six-year-old horse should have all his teeth in wear, and at seven years a hook appears on the upper corner teeth. At eight years of age the hook goes and a fanghole, or central cavity, appears; the cups, or marks, surrounded by a rim of enamel will seem to be larger and the fanghole smaller. At nine years one can judge the age by the cups and fanghole — the cups should be smaller, the fanghole bigger. In the ten-year-old the cups have already disappeared, leaving a fanghole. It is difficult to tell the age of the horse accurately after he is ten years old; the best way to judge is by the angle of the teeth: the older horse appears to have longer teeth because the gums recede.

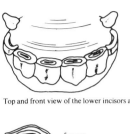

Top and front view of the lower incisors at 5 years

Side view of a horse's mouth at 5 years

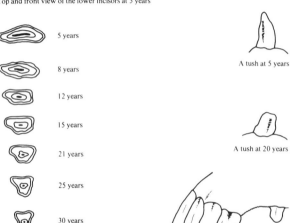

5 years

8 years

12 years

15 years

21 years

25 years

30 years

A tush at 5 years

A tush at 20 years

The changing shape of the teeth showing the 'marks' or 'cups'

Galvayne's groove

Ageing by the teeth

Galvayne's groove appears at approximately ten years of age on the upper corner teeth, is a brownish yellow line, and can be seen half-way down the tooth at around fifteen years. The groove reaches the bottom when the horse is about twenty years old and breaks the surface at twenty-one years. In his thirtieth year the mark disappears from the top and is half way down the tooth.

Bishoping refers to tampering with the teeth to give an old horse a 'young mouth'. Normally a sign of rasping can be found and a false mark is burnt into the tooth (table) with a hot iron or caustic, but as the enamel cannot be restored it is usually possible to get at the truth.

Rising and off are terms used when talking of the age of a horse. A horse that is rising five is nearer five than four years. One that is five off is nearer five than six years.

16 Minor ailments and nursing

Good nursing is tremendously important in the treatment of disease. The skilful groom can do much for the comfort of a sick horse by intelligent and prompt attention to his needs. The ailing animal should be stabled in a well-ventilated box, quite free from draughts. Where several horses are stabled together it is best to keep the sick horse in a box removed from the other horses, where it is possible for him to have quiet and peace away from the bustle of the main yard. A good clean bed of either wheat straw or wood shavings is essential. The stable door must be of a design in which the horse has a half-door, over which he is able to lean his head, especially if he is suffering from a respiratory problem. If the horse has an eye infection the stable should be kept dark, the windows being covered to allow in only the minimum of light. Sometimes the horse may have an injury or wound that requires him to be tied up all the time. In this case it is still best to have the horse in a stable rather than a straight stall, as the air is better able to circulate.

Warmth is also important; the horse should be kept warm by a light woollen blanket, a jute rug and bandages. Any medical treatment that the horse is receiving should be carried out at the same time each day. If the horse is very ill he should not be left alone, as he will be comforted by a friendly presence; if he is seriously ill there is a need for someone in attendance the whole time in case the horse reaches a crisis condition. Fresh water is most necessary for the general improvement of the horse's health. Unfortunately, water left in the stable may become tainted by the fumes of ammonia from the stable, and water buckets must thus be changed frequently.

The sick horse will usually need to be on a laxative diet. Laxative food is easily digested and is non-heating. The horse's strength must be maintained as much as possible by tempting him to eat, as often as he will, small quantities of food that are palatable to him. Do not try to force him to eat. If the horse is running a high temperature then he will very likely not wish to eat. Many horses will take a little skimmed milk diluted with water; as they begin to recover more variety may be introduced to the diet.

The following are all laxative foods which may be found useful additions to a diet: green grass, green oats, lucerne, carrots, apples, linseed and bran mash, boiled barley, gruel, linseed tea, hay tea, milk and eggs. If the horse refuses to eat, do not leave the food in the manger, as this may merely dull the appetite even more. Grooming should be restricted to simple 'quartering' (see page 15). The horse will feel refreshed if he is lighly groomed, but may become excessively tired if you try to strap him. Simply pick out his feet, sponge his eyes, nose and dock, and lightly brush the horse all over. Do not 'bang' him. The following is a very short glossary of the more common medical and veterinary terms.

Abscess: a collection of pus which may be found in any part of the body.

Absorbent: a vessel which takes up various fluids in the body.

Anaemia: a blood deficiency.

Chronic: a disease or illness that lasts a long time before eventual relief, cure or death.

Drench: a drink, usually medicinal, administered to the horse.

Colic: abdominal pain.

Poultice: an application to help remove inflammation and swellings.

If and when you are obliged to read the temperature, pulse or respiration of a horse, you will need an assistant to hold the animal still. When taking the temperature it is advisable first to put a headcollar on the horse. You will need a suitable thermometer, a jar of Vaseline and surgical spirit. Apply plenty of jelly to the end of the thermometer so that it can slip easily into the rectum. Hold it there for two minutes, remove the thermometer and read it. I have found that it is best to keep a daily record of all my horses if I have one horse that I suspect to be ill. In this way I can anticipate trouble and administer treatment immediately. It is useful to tie a

Daily attention to the horse's feet is essential. Here the groom is using a hoof pick to remove dirt from the sole of the foot

It is good practice to take the horse's temperature regularly

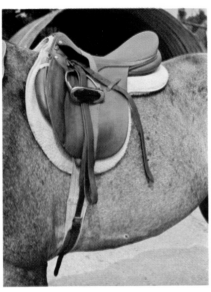

A well-fitting forward-cut saddle suitable for jumping. The surcingle has been fitted to prevent the saddle from slipping

Dressed for travelling, the horse is loaded into the trailer

string to the end of your thermometer, so that you can clip it to the horse's tail and prevent its loss by being sucked in or dropped.

When the reading is completed the thermometer must be cleansed by dipping it into the surgical spirit and wiping it dry. It is of course essential to ensure that the thermometer is below 32°C (90°F) before being used, if necessary by a firm downwards shaking until it is low enough for use. The normal temperature for a horse is about 38°C (100.5°F). The temperature will be slightly higher (about one degree) later in the day and should never be taken immediately after work, when it naturally stays higher for an hour or so.

A reading of the pulse of a horse is normally taken where the submaxillary artery passes under the jaw. Alternatives are the zygomatic artery (the eye), carotid artery (the neck — jugular vein) and the radial artery, which is found at the elbow. The normal pulse rate of a healthy horse is 36–40 beats per minute, small ponies about 45 beats. Normal variations may occur.

The normal respiration rate of a horse is 8–12 per minute. The best way to take a reading is to stand behind the horse and watch the rise and fall of his flanks.

Administering unpalatable powders in feeds

There may be occasions when your horse requires some medical powder or tablet, and it is a good idea to administer this in his feed. Make the feed smaller than usual so you can be certain that the whole feed will be eaten. The content must be particularly palatable, so add apples, carrots, molasses etc., according to the horse's preference, to help disguise the smell of the medicine.

Wounds and their treatment

It is time for a few words on the subject of the treatment of wounds and galls. There are four main types of wound: incised, punctured, lacerated and contused. A sharp instrument, such as a knife or a piece of glass, is normally the cause of an incised or clean-cut wound, usually with considerable early bleeding which

E

stops fairly quickly and is therefore relatively easy to control. Punctured wounds are more difficult to cope with, as they often heal over on the surface thus imprisoning potentially dangerous germs. Lacerated wounds are very painful and are caused by a blunt object or by barbed wire tearing the skin. The surface is rough and there is less bleeding than with an incised wound. Contusions or bruising are the most common type of wound, caused by a blow or kick which does not break the skin.

In the treatment of wounds, fresh air is the best nurse and may be quite sufficient with a small injury as long as the wound is clean. It is always advisable to have the horse injected against tetanus. With a more severe injury the edges of the wound should be brought together carefully and with gentle pressure, or irrigated with fresh cold water. If there is arterial bleeding a tourniquet must be applied between the wound and the heart, but as a last resort and only by a knowledgeable person, as it can result in serious damage. It is easy to recognize arterial blood as it is bright red and flows in sharp spurts. It is essential to consult a veterinary surgeon immediately if arterial bleeding is suspected.

Venous blood flows steadily and is dark red in colour. Blood from a vein may be treated with cold water. The golden rule with punctured wounds is not to probe — a gentle trickle of water from a hosepipe can help cleanse the wound without the handler having to touch the damaged area. It may be necessary for your veterinary surgeon to probe the wound, but it is best if you leave well alone: there is a danger of rupturing the oil sac if the wound is near a joint. If the wound is near a joint it is advisable to call a vet, who will most probably put the horse on a course of antibiotics, a very effective way of treating this type of ailment and puncture wounds as well.

Naturally, the stable must be kept scrupulously clean to avoid any possible risk of infection. If the injury is serious enough for the horse to be off work, he should be put on a laxative diet.

Inflammation

The natural reaction of tissues to an injury or to irritation is inflammation, heat, pain and swelling. An increase in the flow of blood brings food to repair damaged cells and replace those that have died. If the artery walls are damaged, they become more porous and blood oozes out into the damaged area, causing that part to swell. As soon as the flow of blood becomes impeded, stagnation occurs, therefore treatment to ensure good, blood circulation is needed to help and reduce inflammation. Heat is one means of effecting this by relieving the congestion. Fomenting, cold hosing, poulticing and tubbing are other methods used to reduce inflammation. Fomenting is simply the application of a towel that has been immersed in a bucket of hot water. Fill a bucket two-thirds full of boiling water and dip the towel into it, holding onto the ends. Wring out the towel and hold it to the affected area.

Cold treatments to reduce inflammation include the application of ice-cold bandages, or, more effectively, hosing the affected part with cold water. Before cold hosing it is advisable first to rub Vaseline into the horse's heels to avoid chafing, then gently to allow the water to trickle above the knee and run down the leg. You could also cold hose after jumping, working or hard going, as it will take some of the soreness out of the legs.

Poulticing reduces heat and inflammation by the use of direct heat. Bran is the most common form of poultice for the foot. Animalintex or Kaolin are very effective used on other parts of the body. A poultice is best changed every twelve hours so that maximum benefit is obtained from each application.

Tubbing is when you fill a rubber bucket half full of hot, but *not* boiling, water, and put the horse's foot in it, to draw out inflammation. Before immersing the foot in the water, rub Vaseline into the horse's heels.

Colic — its symptoms and treatment

A digestive disturbance inside the horse is known as colic. There are two forms, spasmodic and flatulent (ordinary) colic. The first signs that a horse has colic are easily recognizable. He may repeatedly get up and down, often trying to roll, may paw at the ground, and will look round at his sides, trying to kick them. His coat may be staring, he may even be sweating. In short, he will look generally uncomfortable. One important symptom, present in all cases, is the refusal of the horse to feed. If your horse shows any of the signs described call the vet at once. While you are waiting for the vet to arrive, keep the horse warm with rugs and blankets. Put a headcollar on him and gently walk him about, to prevent him lying down and rolling. It is often thought that a rolling horse may suffer a twisted gut, but there is no direct evidence of this, and it is probable that in most cases the twist causes the rolling. However, it is best to keep the horse upright so that he does not injure himself by becoming cast against a wall or dashing his head on the ground. The vet will probably administer a pain-relieving drug but in severe cases surgery may be necessary.

If the horse is suffering from spasmodic colic, the colic spasms will be intermittent. Colic will appear, then for some time no colic symptoms will be present, then they will reappear. The method of treatment for spasmodic colic is the same as for ordinary colic.

When handling any sick horse remember to be quiet, do not over fuss him, make sure he has all that he needs: fresh water, clean bedding and warmth. Keep a chart for temperature, pulse, and whether he has eaten, or drunk water. Also record how many times he has passed droppings, or staled. If the treatment he has to have is unpleasant and may upset him, get a friend to put on his bridle for control while you hold up a foreleg so he will stand still and make sure the treatment is carried out as quickly and gently as possible.

Injuries and other ailments

Speedy cutting is a problem in which the inside of the near foot hits the offside leg, somewhere on the inside of the knee. Probable causes are faulty conformation, inferior shoeing or poor condition. The most effective prevention is to fit brushing boots or bandages, and of course every effort should be made to improve the horse's balance and condition.

Forging describes the situation which arises when the fore shoe is

84

struck by the toe of the hind shoe. The cause may again be faulty shoeing, or it can be found in an unschooled or unbalanced horse, or one in poor condition. To prevent its happening have the toe of the hind shoe set back a little, and school the horse to improve his movement, being sure never to work him when he is tired.

Over-reach occurs when the toe of the hind shoe strikes the foreleg. A high over-reach is a strike above the fetlock and a low over-reach is below, and is usually the more critical of the two, as it can create a lot of bruising. The accident is most likely to happen while the horse is jumping, or perhaps galloping in going that is too heavy. To prevent its happening, fit over-reach boots and have the toe of the hind shoe rolled.

Brushing occurs when the fetlock joint of the near fore is struck by the foot of the off fore, causing bruising. The problem arises from faulty shoeing and poor conformation in an unbalanced or unschooled horse. Brushing may occur in front or behind; the easiest way to prevent it is to have the horse shod with a feather-edged shoe, and to see that he always wears brushing boots. Schooling will help improve his basic paces and balance.

Bog spavin is one found on the inside and a little to the front of the hock joint. The cause is strain, probably through slipping in heavy going, and the treatment is to rest and blister. It is advisable always to go steadily in heavy going to lessen the risk of a strain.

Bone spavin is found on the inside of the leg, just below the hock joint. The fault is often hereditary, but a horse with cow hocks is more prone to it. Work in heavy going may also be a cause. The treatment is to rest the horse and to raise the heels of the hind shoes. Consult your vet.

Windgalls are to be found on either side and just above the fetlock joint. Again, the cause is strain and hard work. The best way to treat them is to rest the horse and cold hose; the wearing of stable bandages will sometimes help this ailment.

Capped hocks are found on the point of the hock and are caused by lack of bedding or by the horse kicking in the stable. The remedy is to apply a working blister or, better still, use the preventative measure of fitting hock boots for travelling and putting plenty of fresh bedding in the box.

Splints are bony enlargements of the cannon bone, usually found on the inside of the leg, but sometimes on the outside. They are caused by the unnecessary jarring of a horse's legs, through jumping or trotting on hard going, by poor conformation and shoeing and also by a horse knocking itself. The condition is more often found in a horse under six years old. The treatment is to frequently apply cold water or lead lotion bandages to the inflammed area, and to rest your horse. The ideal preventions are to ensure that your horse is properly shod, to see that he wears bandages or boots when schooling, and not to work him on hard going if he is a young horse.

Coughing. Among all ailments there is no doubt that coughing is a very troublesome complaint, partly because once in the stable it is extremely difficult to get rid of. Often it is a symptom of a more serious complaint and sometimes, though not always, it is infectious. There is usually some inflammation, which starts the coughing. While a horse is coughing it is considered to have an unsoundness and must be treated with great care. As soon as a cough is discovered the animal should be isolated, kept warm and out of draughts. The treatment is straightforward, and follows the principles already described. Remember to use rugs and bandages for warmth; take the horse's temperature twice a day; keep the horse on a laxative diet, and perhaps damp his hay to avoid any dust. Sometimes it is beneficial to use a cough electuary, steam the head, and rub liniment on the throat. If the cough persists and the horse runs a high temperature call the vet. Always remember that no horse should be worked fast until he is completely recovered after an illness.

Worms

Horses are susceptible to worms and it is advisable to know the different types, the symptoms, likely causes and treatment.

Redworm Symptoms: the horse eats well but suffers loss of flesh, dry dull coat, dull eye, and possibly diarrhoea. The worm is rarely visible in the droppings; general debility and anaemia may follow. Cause: usually picked up from the field where a number of horses may be at grass together. Treatment: seek your vet's advice about a suitable worming programme and diet. The horse will need to be put on a very nutritious diet to help build him up.

Stomach bots Symptoms: the horse will eat plenty but does not seem to put on flesh and has a dry staring coat; the bot may sometimes be seen in the droppings. Cause: the horse licks his legs, on which the yellow eggs have been laid, and swallows them; they will then hatch in the stomach. Treatment: if noticed on the legs, the eggs should be clipped off and a worm powder given. There are several worming preparations available which are effective against bots and your vet will be able to advise you.

Round worm Symptoms: very few — the horse may have a few attacks of colic or irregular bowel movements. Cause: often picked up on stale pasture. Treatment: it is best to call the vet and follow his advice.

Whipworm Symptoms: the horse will rub his tail and a yellow discharge will appear on the dock. Treatment: some forms of worm powder will deal with this, but if you are in doubt, consult your vet. This type of worm is only found in the rectum.

Respiratory problems

A small group of closely related respiratory problems are known as whistling, roaring and broken wind.

Whistling is a high-pitched noise which the horse makes in his throat.

Roaring is a noise similar to that of whistling and also a result of a breakdown of the muscle or a blockage on the larynx.

Broken wind, on the other hand, is a breakdown of the air vesicles of the lungs. The important difference is that whistling and roaring are in the throat, whereas broken wind is a condition of the lungs.

Sprains

Some mention has already been made of sprains and strains, but it is worth considering them in more detail. Strains take place in tendon and ligaments. A tendon is an extension from a muscle and links the muscle to bone (the upper muscle, called belly muscle, has more elasticity and will not sprain as easily as a tendon). A ligament, however, though made of hard fibres like a tendon, has a different function: it holds one or more bones together, or supports a joint. It does not have the resilient 'belly' and is therefore less elastic. Ligaments link bone to bone, except for the check ligament which runs from the knee to the perforans tendon.

Strained tendons are generally caused by working the horse fast when he is exhausted or unfit, by galloping on soft or boggy ground, or by jumping out of or into mud, especially at drop fences. This is why so many event horses break down; the jar and concussion to which the forelegs are subjected when the horse is jumping big drop fences is tremendous, and the animal therefore needs to be as fit as any racehorse to compete successfully and remain sound. Pulling up suddenly, or slipping, could also result in a strain. The symptoms will be heat, pain, swelling and lameness — not too much, perhaps, in a slightly sprained tendon though a severe strain will cause considerable lameness and pain. The best way to treat this ailment is to stop all work and put the horse on a laxative diet. Consult your vet, who will probably tell you to foment and poultice with kaolin to relieve the pain and draw blood to the area, which will help the healing process and decrease the amount of swelling, thus improving the circulation. Do not exercise your horse, but keep him in the stable with a support bandage on the sound leg and a poultice on the strained leg. Under your vet's advice, continue poulticing for three to four days, after which call the vet if there is no improvement. Your vet may advise you to continue poulticing for a further week, and suggest that you shoe with a wedge-heel shoe. After poulticing, cold-water hose the affected area. Depending on the severity of the strain the horse may need from six to as much as eighteen months rest before healing is completed. Of course, when the animal comes into work again, he must begin with walking exercise for at least three weeks, advancing to trot work gradually, on a progressive fittening programme.

The suspensory ligament is attached to the cannon bone behind the knee, and runs down the back of the cannon bone between the two splint bones. Just above the sesamoid bone it divides into four strands, its function being to hold the fetlock joint in its suspended position and help support the tendons. A strain is normally developed slowly with general wear or fast work on hard ground. The usual sign to watch for is a shortening of the stride, although the horse will not be lame. If, however, the strained ligament is complicated by ruptured tendons, then the whole lot can break down, producing tremendous swelling over the entire area. If it is just strained there may be some swelling around the tendon area, but there will not be a bow. A bow means that the horse has broken down and that there is a rupture of the suspensory ligament and tendon. To treat the suspensory, it is best to poultice with kaolin to reduce the inflammation. Poultice for about a week and then, on the advice of a vet, have the horse turned out for six weeks. The horse will not need as long a rest as after a sprained tendon.

The check ligament is found at the back of the knee, to halfway down the cannon bone, where it joins the perforans tendon and acts as a support to it. A strain to this ligament may be caused by tiredness and heavy or deep going. There will be heat, pain, some swelling and lameness. The treatment is similar to that for other strained ligaments: rest the horse, poultice and blister.

17   Stable tricks and vices

Kicking in the stable

This can be a very annoying habit and is normally caused through enforced idleness and general boredom, or because of parasites, such as heel bug, rats or mice in the stable. The best way to cope with the problem is to pad the stable with matting or foam rubber. Be sure to keep the horse well exercised, ensuring that he has no opportunity to become bored by dividing his exercise periods into two or three sessions daily instead of the usual one.

Stamping and pawing

This is very often caused simply by impatience at feed time, though it could be the sign of an attack of colic. Sometimes the habit may develop as a result of boredom in the stable, and again it is a good idea to divide the exercise periods. At feed times if there is more than one horse try to deal with all the horses as quickly as possible so that none are kept waiting too long.

Biting and snapping

Biting is very often the result of poor grooming; a sensitive horse will be irritated by rough and improper handling when groomed. The perpetual feeding of titbits is also a sure way of teaching the horse to snap. If you have this problem with a horse, treat it always with firmness and kindness; tie up a confirmed biter for grooming or close handling; be careful not to irritate the ticklish horse. Hand grooming is better than employing a rather rough brush. A firm slap on the muzzle will often achieve satisfactory results if the habit has only just started.

Crib-biting and wind-sucking

These are far more serious vices than those previously mentioned, and sufficiently serious to constitute an unsoundness when the horse is under veterinary inspection. A crib-biter takes hold of any projection in the box or stable with his incisor teeth and swallows in air. Serious damage may result to the incisor teeth, causing the horse to experience difficulty in grazing. A wind-sucker arches his neck, swallowing air without biting on anything. In both cases the swallowing of the air may cause colic, and affect the digestion to such a degree that the horse may well have difficulty in keeping weight on. Crib-biters and wind-suckers also often begin their vice through boredom, sometimes coupled with insufficient bulk feed such as hay, chaff or grass. To prevent this vice, the remedy is again to divide your exercise programme so that the horse has plenty to interest him. Try also to stable a crib-biter in a stall with no surfaces for him to crib on. Correct the diet so that there is an adequate supply of bulk food available. Isolate a horse with this problem, as other horses in the stable may imitate it. In severe cases a wide strap attached round the slim portion of the neck and fastened securely enough to prevent the muscles contracting will assist in the curing of wind-sucking.

Weaving

A horse that weaves rocks from side to side in his stable, never able to relax or rest, the forelegs and head rocking to and fro. This vice is also warranted as an unsoundness, and may be termed a nervous vice as well as one that is caused through boredom. Certain horses will only weave when the groom is in the stable, but confirmed weavers will do it all the time, so much so that they may even become lame. Weaving is another case in which boredom must be avoided at all costs, by division of the exercise periods. Always have available a good, deep bed which will encourage the horse to rest and lie down. A weight, such as a brick, a piece of wood or tyres, suspended over the top of the door can be effective, as the horse will knock into it as he weaves.

The horse that does not like to lie down

The usual cause of preferring to stand is that the horse has insufficient bedding and is therefore worried about injuring himself. Old horses are also often reluctant to lie down, as they fear that it may be difficult to get up again. Horses obviously rest much more if they will lie down, so ensure that you have a deep bed: this will help the horse's limbs to remain supple much longer.

Eating the bedding

Many young horses eat their bed and it is normally as a result of boredom, insufficient bulk food, worms, or the lack of mineral salts. Divide the exercise periods daily, give plenty of bulk food, plus mineral salts. Mix the new bedding with the used bedding, damp the whole with disinfectant. If the horse persists, bed him down on shavings or shredded paper.

Dealing with a 'cast' horse

The term 'cast' is used when the horse has rolled violently in his stable and is lying with his body against a wall, with all four legs in the air in such a position that he is unable to lift himself to his feet. Enter the stable, speaking calmly to reassure the horse that all is well. Immediately call for help, sit on the neck just behind the head to keep him still and prevent his panicking. Remove all buckets, haynets and so forth, and if possible remove or undo the rugs. You will require two lunge lines or a good length of rope. Put the lunge lines around all four legs, arranging them high up the leg so they will not slip, and allow greater leverage. Then ask the person sitting on the head to rise and talk quietly to the horse. With your assistant, pull the horse over and when he is upright again, check for any injuries. Be careful in dealing with a cast horse, since he may thrash and struggle and possibly cause injury to his would-be rescuers. If your horse is inclined to get cast, fit an anti-cast roller, and ensure at all times that he has a good deep bed with the sides well banked up.

18 Travelling routines

There is a routine preparation for the loading and unloading of horses travelling by road, rail and air. If the best results are to be achieved from your young horse as a competitor or as a hunter it is important that he becomes accustomed to transport and is relaxed and undisturbed both by the loading into the vehicle and by the actual journey. It is preferable to teach a young horse to load at home, long before you wish to take him on a journey, either by feeding him in the trailer or by loading another horse first and letting him follow. Take him for a short drive, for about five minutes only, so that he realizes there is nothing to fear. However, you may not have your horse as a youngster and may need to teach him to load easily when he is a mature animal.

Loading

Here are some pointers on loading for the inexperienced handler:

1 Position the horsebox or trailer (if you can at first use a spacious box, rather than a narrow trailer, so much the better) next to a hedge or in a gateway where a natural wing will be provided. Place the ramp on an incline so that the angle of entry to the trailer is slight. If possible, have the sun shining *into* the trailer so the horse can see easily.
2 Have a feed and haynet ready, open the windows and ventilators for more light. You will need a lunge line or rope, and an assistant.
3 Put a headcollar on the horse, with a bridle on top. The horse should be dressed with travelling equipment consisting of a tail bandage, stable bandages, knee boots, and a rug.
4 Walk confidently in a straight line towards the vehicle, being

Travelling boots. These are a useful alternative to the stable
bandage to protect the legs while travelling

careful not to hesitate or rush the horse. Try to remain close to
his shoulder, without looking back or getting in front of him.

5 Having walked with the horse right inside the box, ask your
assistant to attach the rear strap quickly so that the horse cannot
reverse out of the box. Tie up the horse, removing the bridle at
the same time. Allow him sufficient room to eat his hay, but not
so much that he is able to turn round or bite his neighbour!

You may sometimes come across a horse that is reluctant to
load: the following hints may be helpful to you. Certain horses are
so nervous and tense that they will not look at the box or even
approach it. If this should be the case you must take your time and
try never to load the horse if you yourself are in a hurry, as you
will only frighten him more. Encourage him with a feed, handling
him firmly and quietly. If possible, put the horse in long reins and
drive him into the box. If the horse is fully encased between the
trainer and the reins, and you have an efficient assistant to do up
the backstrap quickly when you are in the box, you will find that
this method is nearly always successful.

Another type of problem that can be experienced is that of the horse who stands at the edge of the ramp and will go no further, swinging his quarters and jumping off the ramp. You should wait until you have the horse standing quietly in front of the ramp, then take a lunge line behind him, placing it above the hocks and under the tail. With gentle pressure on the line the horse should move away and go forward into the box. If this does not work, try loading another horse first, as there is a possibility that the difficult horse will follow.

Try regularly loading the horses that are difficult to handle, feeding them in the box when it is stationary, so that they begin to treat the box as though it were another stable.

The journey

During a journey the driver should be careful to give the horse as comfortable a ride as possible, changing gear often, using all the gears and driving slowly, especially on corners. It is stupid to give the horse a valid reason for being afraid of travelling.

Remember that a journey is tiring for you and can be even more tiring for your horse, so if you wish him to go well for you, see that he is driven well and carefully, allowing plenty of time.

Unloading

Unloading is just as important as loading. Do not hustle or hurry your horse in any way; *be sure to untie him* before you release the breeching strap if he is coming out backwards, or alternatively the breast strap if he is coming out forwards. Partitions in horse boxes and trailers are almost always a little on the narrow side, so watch the horse's hips carefully, and do not allow him to bang them. Carelessness in this matter may result in the horse refusing to unload, or perhaps rushing out and injuring himself. It goes without saying that the ramp must have matting of some sort so that the horse does not slip.

Glossary of American Equivalents

Animalintex *a poultice. Alternatives are antiphlogisten or numotizine*
Broken wind *respiratory condition known as 'heaves'*
Buffer *clench cutter*
Corn *grain*
Crib-biting *cribbing*
Day rug *blanket or sheet*
Dumping *dubbing*
Dustbin *garbage can*
Headcollar *halter*
Humour spots *feed bumps*
Jute rug *thick blanket, made of hessian or hemp with a woollen lining*
Kimblewick *Tom Thumb, a small mild curb bit*
Loose-box *box-stall*
Meadow hay *grass hay*
Nuts *pellets*
Over-reach boots *bell-boots*

Pincers *pinchers or nippers*
Plaiting *braiding*
Racehorse cubes *pellets*
Ragwort *a poisonous plant. Plants to be avoided: cheet grass, loco weed and larkspur*
Rasping *floating*
Rubbish *garbage*
Rug and rugging up *blanket and blanketing*
Running reins *draw reins*
Seed hay *alfalfa*
Skep *manure basket*
Spade *shovel*
Spanner *wrench*
Stockinette *cotton-knit, used for bandaging*
Sweat-rug *cooler, an over-sized blanket specially designed for cooling and drying-out*
Tap *faucet*

Acknowledgments

We are particularly indebted to Mrs Hatton-Hall F.B.H.S. for all her kindness, help and encouragement; to Miss Marie Stokes F.B.H.S. for her assistance and technical advice, and for allowing her horses and facilities at Walton Heath Livery Stables to be used for the photographs; to Candida Geddes for the benefit of her knowledge and careful observation in the preparation of this book; to Bob Targett whose photographs have so enriched this publication; and to Peter Landon for additional black and white photographs.